NEW BRUNSWICK, NEW JERSEY, GOODBYE

BANDS, DIRTY BASEMENTS, AND THE SEARCH FOR SELF

RONEN KAUFFMAN

New Brunswick, New Jersey, Goodbye
Published by Hopeless Records/Sub City Records
P.O Box 7495 Van Nuys, CA 91409, U.S.A.

Edited by Randy Kershner

Photos by Zak Kaplan unless otherwise noted

Layout & Design by Zak Kaplan – roguestatedesign.com
Typesetting by C. Spliedt – plasticfly.com

First Edition

0 1 2 3 4 5 6 7 8 9

ISBN: 978-0-9677287-4-2

A number of people had to be harassed regarding this memoir. They are, in
no particular order: Starr James, Louis Posen, Ian Harrison and everyone
at Hopeless/SubCity, Carl Severson, Zak Kaplan, Asim Shaikh, Randy
Kershner, Daniel Wharton, Chad Renshaw, Frank Iero, Ross Seigel, Richard
Cohn, Marc Schapiro, Dan Yemin, Chris Ross, Benny Horowitz, Jason
Small, Chris Spliedt, Allison Salenteri, Steve Asbury, Pedro Angel Serrano,
Rob Hitt, Peter Ventantonio, Jack Terricloth, Matt Leveton, Paul Hanly, Kate
Hiltz, Matthew Hay, and Guav. Extra thanks to those friends who answered
questions and tolerated me.

Official MySpace page: myspace.com/hubcitybook
Ronen Kauffman's website: kamikazewords.com
Hopeless Records: hopelessrecords.com

This is SC036.

For my wife, Starr James,
for her endless patience, support, help, and love;
for my parents, Aliza and Bruce Kauffman,
for the cells, the love, and everything else.
Also, for the kids.

CONTENTS

FOREWORD

"Hub City Ricochet" is what we used to call it. Kids hit this town, bounce off the walls, into each other, make an impact. They form or put on bands, make the scene, pack Basements, sell out Scott Hall, get one of the college bars to do an all ages show and then come to that crux: use their momentum to achieve escape velocity, or start bartending at The Court Tavern. Well, I shouldn't be one to judge. I did my time there as well.

New Brunswick is an exciting place - the college provides a constant influx of new faces, ideas, and music, music everywhere. The rent is cheap and if you are of a certain age it is easy to sneak into the campus dining facilities. That is the one major difference between myself and the protagonist of the memoir you are about to read: I never went to Rutgers; I actually grew up in the town so I was used to seeing the Mason Gross students appear, age and fall away. First they were older, then contemporaries, then eager looking kids and it was definitely time to go. And The Big City always loomed there - at times something we longed to be taken seriously in, and at times something we defined ourselves against. I remember when CB's matinees got too dunder-headed for young spiky haired kids to hang out at without getting in fistfights with SOD fans who didn't like "peace punks". We decided, "We can put on shows in our own state and you kids from Long Island can have the Lower East Side." I like to think that is when The Brunfis scene started up. And there were always bands. I could list them off as Ronen lists off the ones he came up with in the following pages, but the names don't mean so much to anybody who wasn't there - I don't recognize most of the bands he talks about. But what I do recognize in these pages are the people who make them up; I recognize the scene. It never was - thank goodness - the music that defined us. It's our hope, our outrage at limited options, our yearning for more than what is offered - our demand to write our own rules, to tell our own story. That's the thread that runs through these punk rock communities in B-cities of maligned states. That, and our tendency to cling to each other searching for antecedents to our spectacularly bad ideas while avoiding any thought of the future. Our headlong flight into that cruel windshield: stay in the place you've become comfortable in, or continue the adventure that brought you there in the first place? What are you gonna do with that momentum? Settle or dare?

Here's the way we used to dare each other back in Jersey; it may sound silly but I hear it in the back of my mind everyday: "Fate loves the fearless." Fuck yeah.

Up the punks.

Jack Terricloth
World/Inferno Friendship Society
Brooklyn, NY by way of New Brunswick, NJ
1/20/07

4

*"Writing is not necessarily something to be ashamed of,
but do it in private and wash your hands afterwards."*

- Robert Heinlein (1907 - 1988)

NEW BRUNSWICK, NEW JERSEY, GOODBYE

Preface

The crowd often finds it fishy when a single person tries to define a collective experience; even more so if it's an attempt to define punk or hardcore. So while reading this book, be advised: it is not a historical text – nor a complete record of what happened in the New Brunswick hardcore punk scene from 1994-2000. This is a story about me and my experiences in a town in New Jersey – a selective re-telling of some memories, confirmed through informal interviews and research. In an attempt to apply some kind of meaningful continuity to my blabbering, I've even chosen to omit some friends, bands, shenanigans and subtexts all together – not because they lack importance; just because.

Consequently, many will finish this book and conclude that my experiences with music and people were nothing like their own. That's how it should be, of course - whether because of some punk rock mumbo jumbo about individualism, or because diversity is good for nature, or because it's just plain impossible for any two people's lives to be exactly the same. Variety is the spice of life, and so on.

Most people hear the word "autobiography" and think of someone writing the story of his or her own life. But *any* writing done by an individual tells part of that person's life story. Each of us, with our own unique set of experiences and perspective, writes what we know. Blatantly or between the lines, consciously or not – writing usually says more than what it… says.

Of course, most people don't write more than what's required by school, work, or daily living. Lucky for them, reading is autobiographical, too.

That's because everything you read passes through that same unique lens, ground from the circumstance and physiology of your own particular life. This means that no one can read these words the way you are reading them right now. No one can hear that song and feel it the way you do. It's like food – you can't eat a grape and have someone else digest it for you. Once that grape was chewed and swallowed, you committed to processing it. The same goes for all art. Once you put your eyes or ears to something, the digestion in your brain is your job and no one else's. And ultimately, this leaves you just as responsible as your favorite band, actor, or writer for whether or not you connect with their art. Like most things in life, you only get back when you put in.

For now, human beings seem hopelessly mired in subjectivity, even despite countless pursuits of enlightenment. To me, that's always been pretty depressing. But limitations are not an excuse for not trying in life - so long ago I decided that I really could make my time interesting, and important, and worthy of stories people would want to hear. Like Henry David Thorough told me in high school, I chose to live deep and suck the marrow from life. And in the end, the way I did this was through music.

One - My Media Obsession

As far back as I can remember, I was obsessed with media.

Take second grade, for example, when fellow 7-year-old Jeff Sassinsky and I decided to start an independent newspaper at Beeler Elementary in Marlton, New Jersey. Or the comic book club I formed at age 11; there were two members – me, and my best friend Chad, who lived two doors down. We saw each other all day, every day – but nonetheless needed a newsletter so urgently that *The Rag* got all the way to issue #2 before it fizzled. I wouldn't say I was crushed. I was 11.

But my media fixation persisted. Over the years, I sampled the options - school newspapers; literary magazines; even a yearbook. All good fun, I suppose; and great experience, too. That is, with just one problem – I never felt *satisfied*. Seeing my name in print was cool, and making media was cool, but without some sort of real-world impact it meant nothing to me. I knew that I wanted something deeper and better; even today, I have a difficult time describing this feeling. Still, it was there; in my head and in my heart - intangible, inexplicable, and completely real. Some might call that kind of experience "God," or maybe a hallucination. I didn't call it anything. I just went with it. As far as feelings go, it was, after all, so strong and certain.

My first "serious" attempt at channeling this impulse came during my sophomore year of high school. It was a short-lived underground school newspaper called *Propaganda*, which consisted of 1) predictable but well-conceived diatribes against school policies, 2) bad poetry with curse words that the school literary magazine refused to print, and 3) stolen Peter Bagge comic strips. Not surprisingly, the publication's existence was brief. By issue two, my few contributors had all flaked out; worse, the shit was starting to hit the fan in school. I'd dodged a few teachers' questions about the project, but was eventually called down to the principal's office. The authorities told me, of course, that I couldn't associate a publication with the school; also, that I couldn't distribute publications in school, and that if I didn't stop it would be a problem. I was 15 years old, and I didn't want to get in trouble. *Propaganda* was done.

Chad (from two doors down) and I had remained best friends throughout our school years; and where we had once convened over comic books and ghost stories, our teen years were dominated by one basic interest: music. Over time, we immersed ourselves in everything we could find – admittedly, stumbling over a few honkers along the way. For example, I definitely owned (and enjoyed) Europe's *The Final Countdown*; Chad was briefly into Tony! Toni! Toné! and Another Bad Creation.

But despite lapses in judgment, we often picked winners. Consequently, our youth became almost exclusively defined by the constant uncovering of new listening material. Now clearly, the teen years are *the* time of discovery, exploring identity, and all that stuff – but that's easy for any adult to say. Back then, our love of music was an impulse that came from deep in our so-called souls – a powerful and seemingly necessary aspect of daily life. Music was like food or air, and we'd dig up bands like they were buried treasures – often finding fool's gold. But the scattered gems we did find ultimately proved precious – Queen, Iron Maiden, N.W.A., Public Enemy and Faith No More were a few of them. We loved Helmet and Metallica. And though our tastes weren't always the same – I liked Morrisey while Chad liked Ween, for example – we agreed most of the time; this meant that we could look to one another as trusted sources of new music.

But at the time it seemed much simpler than that.

It was, after all, the early 90s – a period that couldn't have been more bountiful when it came to new music. And 1989 and '90 were so unabashedly permissive when it came to what records succeded. Remember, the mainstream was just coming off of acts like Nelson and Wilson Phillips when Nirvana swooped in to shift the paradigm in 1991.

That isn't to under cut the many bands that had been providing excellent, enjoyable, *accessible* alternatives to mainstream rock throughout the late 80s – The Cure, Ministry, Ned's Atomic Dustbin and so many more were what made me want to watch *120 Minutes* on MTV. But none of those bands had been able to affect mainstream popular culture the way Nirvana did.

We all know the story. Almost instantly, this single band seemed to make clowns out of the era's biggest rock stars. Bands like Poison and Mötley Crüe were fucked – their approach and apparent values rendered unfashionable in the new mass pop culture, they were all but buried by MTV. Sebastian Bach's gargantuan good looks and Axl Rose's spandex – once slam dunks - were now liabilities. Decadence and glamour were rendered passé, or embarrassing; even less flamboyant acts like Extreme and Mr. Big were now finished. And as for fans – well, they'd seen the light, and couldn't look back. They began to seek bands that offered more "relevant," reality-based music – even if those bands were a little homely. Or a lot. Either way, self-important rock was over, or so it seemed - and to the forefront came the disillusion and angst of alternative, and the newest accidental genre – grunge.

Pearl Jam. Say what you want, but facts are facts: plenty of today's hippest hipsters will admit to totally loving *Ten* when it was first released.

Toward the end of 1993 Chad was listening to a call-in radio show called *Rockline*, and the guest was none other than Pearl Jam vocalist Eddie Vedder. During the interview, Vedder commented about his love for punk music. He talked about his own involvement with the punk scene, and dropped some names - specifically, The Damned and Rollins Band.

So like any obsessive teenager, Chad subsequently went to the music store in the local mall for some punk rock records - specifically, of course, anything by The Damned or Rollins Band. But the record store clerk, in a moment of inspired retail wisdom, told Chad that while they did, indeed, have a Rollins Band record, he might prefer a different stripe of punk bands. They had names like Operation Ivy, Jawbreaker, and Green Day; most of them came from a localized scene in California, and none of their records were available at the mall.

It was a fateful moment.

With Christmas approaching, Chad asked the clerk for the longest list of bands he could muster. Said list was then forwarded almost immediately to Chad's girlfriend, who in turn worked wonders to procuring these hard-to-find CDs. By December, they had all arrived.

Just like that, there was this stack of punk rock CDs - their contents a complete mystery to us. And with hours of new music to explore, going through and discovering the meat of these mysterious punk rock records would take some time if it were to be done properly. Songs would be played, lyrics read and considered, layouts examined and analyzed. When it came to music, we were quite serious.

The first CD from the stack to get our attention was Green

Day's *Kerplunk*. Having been immersed in grave solemnity by many of our favorite bands, Green Day was immediately different. They projected grim sentiments like anger and sadness with a breathtaking brightness. Something about their approach made the musical experience so much more tenable than what we'd been used to – whether it was the tone of the lyrics, or the character of the recording, or the deceptively simple lure of a few major chords set against a 4/4 time signature. Chad and I loved Tool, and we loved Pantera – but we didn't *identify* with those bands. Maybe, it seemed, we'd really never identified with *any* band. Until now.

Don't get me wrong. I'd heard Suicidal Tendencies, Fugazi, The Ramones, and a bunch of other punk bands throughout my younger years. For example, I first learned about the Bad Brains from my cousin Stuart as we sat in a limo at the head of our grandmother's funeral procession. But whether it was a function of age or access, I just never took the time to see what these bands and their songs were really saying – or what set any of them apart from other music I already knew.

And so when another record from Chad's stack became a catalyst for change – well *I* changed.

It was a Sunday afternoon and I was sitting in my room when the phone rang; it was Chad, asking if he could come over. This was unusual, since we almost always met up and hung out at his house and not mine. Nonetheless, he walked into my room minutes later and handed me a CD in its case. Chad firmly instructed me to play it right away, and to read along with the lyrics. And he stood there as I sat cross-legged on the red carpet, listening and reading.

What followed was something new and powerful – a real exchange between me and this music; it felt… balmy; the type of moment in which time stops, perceptions change, and one realizes that something *important* is happening. The closest thing I can compare it to is the sensation I've had while in the moment of a car accident; a confluence of events and chance that makes the physical world seem to stop and pulse, if just for that instant. It is the sensation of a miracle, or a catastrophe. It is otherworldly.

By this point, I'd explored the various counter-cultures available throughout my suburban high school and had emerged feeling savvy. I liked George Carlin and considered myself smarter than the "popular" kids. I had long hair, went to White Zombie concerts, and loved the *Judgment Night* soundtrack. But here was a single record – music and words - arresting me like never before. Every last detail blew me away – from the content to the tone to the explosive, passionate delivery. Suddenly, all of my other records were irrelevant – and from that moment on, I knew that punk rock was for me.

Now that I was into punk rock, I pulled a somewhat predictable 180 when it came to stuff like the school literary magazine. I had, of course, determined that publications like these were Trojan Horses sent by "the man" to keep our minds off of what was *really* going on.

Around the same time, I encountered my first real fanzines. They had names like *Monkeybars*, *Powerline* and *Silly Puddy*, and when they first came into my possession I poured over them endlessly. Furiously. Everything about fanzines hit me like a ton of bricks – the content, the creativity, the passion - these hand-made documents seemed so real, important, and made with love. They were raw, and solely of their creators - not part of the mass culture machine I was beginning to understand and resent. And fanzines were underground; you had to know where to get them and they had to come into your physical possession – especially since the internet had yet to explode. These publications felt special.

But perhaps most striking was that each fanzine seemed so drastically different from the next. *This* one was almost entirely comics and words drawn stylishly by hand, while *that* one was neatly printed interviews with bands, and ads for records. Another was all photos of kids skateboarding. One more offered a mix of Christian messages and record reviews. These guerilla publications were all so far apart from one another, yet remarkably similar.

My media obsession drooled and panted, like a crazed sex maniac. Something clicked, and I realized that I, too, could create something like this. I got to work, and chose the name *Aneurysm*.

Right from the start, I was hooked. I could say whatever I wanted, however I wanted to say it, and I didn't have to depend on the context – or market – of my ridiculous school or any other entity to justify my work. It was an intoxicating and empowering blank slate, and it motivated me like nothing before. I longed for my work to be a soul-pulling experience – to make an impact, and do it with substance. Sure, there was fun to be had - but my first priority was that *Aneurysm* had some kind of real meaning. Obviously, my personal understanding of "meaning" would change considerably over time – but I was always seeking it.

Perhaps in celebration of it being my first issue, *Aneurysm* #1 consisted of a single piece of 8.5"x11" letter paper, photocopied on both sides; it was pretty much a newsletter. The majority of the content was typed out on a manual typewriter, and the rest was done with a pen. Regrettably, *Aneurysm* #2 didn't offer any improvements in terms of layout or design, but it did have twice the content of its predecessor. This time, perhaps in celebration of it being the second issue, the zine consisted of *two* pages of letter paper, photocopied – this time, with a staple.

Those first two issues were total crap. Don't get me wrong; I wrote or printed the occasional stinker well after my initial attempts. But looking back on those early editions makes me cringe - partially for the immaturity in my writing, and partially for my taste in music.

But we all have to start somewhere. So in those initial pages, I covered hippie bands from my high school, and allowed a contributor to un-ironically use the word "fag" in an editorial. So the beginnings of *Aneurysm* – well, they were humble to say the least.

Things started to get more exciting when the local record store agreed to take some of my zines on consignment. Not only was it cool to have my work in a real store frequented by people who might actually be interested – but now I was somewhat more free to distribute copies in school. If a teacher asked where they were coming from, I could just say that people got them from a store and were bringing them into school of their own accord.

I was emboldened, and decided that t was time to get my zines into peoples' hands. I casually gave them to friends at lunch. I had cronies from other grades and classes take bunches and distribute them throughout the school day. In my school of about 1200 students, I quickly made it so that *Aneurysm* was everywhere, and anyone could get a copy - if they knew whom to ask.

To my delight and relief, I wasn't laughed out of the building. I even got a number of positive responses from people who were essentially strangers. People were reading, and they liked it – even if they didn't quite get the whole punk rock thing.

The heat was now officially on, and I knew that I had to keep the interest and momentum going. And so with its third issue, *Aneurysm* became a "half-size" zine - a few sheets of letter paper, folded and stapled to form a booklet. I now had 16 pages, not including the covers – lots of room for all kinds of content. And the new format created a more magazine-like experience for the reader. Many zines of the day were made this way, and so I had lots of examples to follow when it came to exploiting the format. I refined the layout and used an electric typewriter instead of the old manual one. I even used my Commodore 64 to print the word "aneurysm" for the cover. There were a few ads – I ran them for free, of course; but they were real ads for real records, other cool zines, and the local record store. And as I read all the other fanzines as I could find (especially *Maximum RockandRoll, HeartattaCk,* and *Slug and Lettuce*), the content of my own publication started to become more unified, increasingly reflecting my fast-growing identification with punk and hardcore.

Until this point, my media obsession had been a raw block of wood, out of which I'd never really carved anything. But now I was beginning to shape this block, revealing the first faint outlines of a vision that had been with me for some time. I chiseled with words and shaved with images. My confidence grew. Splinters fell to the floor, and the raw block before me started to change shape; the image that began to emerge was *Aneurysm.*

If nothing else, it was further than I had ever gotten before. *Aneurysm* now cost fifty cents, and I was selling copies at punk and hardcore shows throughout southern New Jersey and Philadelphia. When graduation rolled around, I was up to issue #5 and Chad from two doors down was the Assistant Editor.

By the summer of 1994, high school was over forever - and all I cared about was punk rock.

Two – 1994-1995: Tinsley Hall

I probably should have been more excited about finishing high school, especially considering my growing distrust of structure, authority and the infamous "system." Some might even say that high school itself is the epitome of all the things a burgeoning punk rocker should hate, and that I should have been doing some sort of joy-related dance. And yet, I couldn't find it in myself to get even the least bit excited about the next step – college. All I saw were more classes, more morons, more bullshit; none of it was very appealing. But it was the plan I had made, and I didn't have anything better lined up – so I followed through. I'd say I was totally indifferent, but that wouldn't be the whole picture; somehow, I was able to be both apathetic and judgmental at the same time. Either way, one fact was indisputable: college was something to do. *And* – and this was crucial – it was a guaranteed way to move out of my parents' house.

They knew that I was determined to escape, of course – I didn't make a secret of my lust for the notion of living under a different (unsupervised) roof. Looking back, my folks seemed to accept this impulse of mine with a lot of grace and understanding - but they didn't want me to move too far away. So with little effort or real consideration for what I wanted to do academically (a.k.a. nothing), Rutgers was presented to me as what one might call an "executive recommendation." It was, after all, nearby; a good school; and relatively inexpensive - a "perfect" fit. In reality, I don't think I cared at all; but at 18 I was at least somewhat typical - I desperately yearned to be on my own. So if college was the way to go, awesome. As long as I was able to go to punk shows, work on *Aneurysm*, and maybe start a band.

Considerations like these, in fact, did give Rutgers one very compelling aspect: location. New Brunswick, NJ was *full* of music. It was mystical to me. And at the time, I was idealistic - really *into* my anger. To me, being pissed off was art. I considered myself to be much more than just another emotional teenager; more than just a kid going through growing pains. In my mind, I was a practitioner of a deliberate and highly purposed social reaction – a mental and psychological kung-fu used to fend off an insane and antagonistic world. The lifestyle I newly emulated or adopted was, *in itself*, an attempt at making some type of statement. In my mind, I was a walking war cry. And what I wanted more than anything was to be around a robust community of people I could consider to be my cultural peers. I saw New Brunswick as possibly being able to offer this to me - so I applied, enthusiastically, to Rutgers. I applied like a motherfucker.

In fact, I was so sold on New Brunswick that I didn't apply to any other colleges. In the event that Rutgers didn't want me, I was prepared to come up with an alternate plan for, like, life and shit. But it turned out, as I had expected, that I didn't need that alternate plan. I was headed to New Brunswick in the fall – the acceptance letter said so.

On a beautiful day in May of 1994, Rutgers held orientation for the incoming class of 1998. School wasn't starting for a few months, but this was a first encounter with my new "peers" - and I wanted to maximize any opportunities for "punkness" to occur.

I wore my Operation Ivy shirt that day. It was a beacon.

The shirt helped me meet Tweety. We were both filling out bubble sheets in a room full of kids when he chatted me up. His first words to me were a magical question: "Do you like punk rock?" Within seconds, he was plugging his band - Heidnik Stew; and within minutes, he'd asked if I wanted to be his roommate. I told Tweety that I already had one lined up. I was lying.

But let's take a step back.

Tweety was big – but more of a 'big dude' than a 'fat guy.' He had a large safety pin through his ear lobe – let's describe the pin as "not new." On his fingers, he wore roughly half a dozen death metal rings; you know, chrome demon skulls with fangs, minotaurs with flaming horns – that sort of thing. He often sported purple or brown calf-length Cross Colors brand shorts, with his trademark Tweety Bird suspenders. Tweety had long, scraggly sideburns, and his Mohawk tapered to a point at his front hairline, gradually fanning outward so that from behind, he was a long-hair. On his feet, 8-eye Doc Martens boots in "cherry smooth," but he called them "ox blood." And while many punk rockers of the time had chains attached to their wallets, most didn't use the heavy industrial kind the way Tweety did. Somehow, it matched the rest of him – the "cling-clang" let you know he was coming from a quarter-mile away.

But despite his outrageous appearance, what really made Tweety impossible to ignore was his personality. He was positively vigorous, even when dead tired. When speaking, Tweety was emphatic, animated and unavoidable; and although he did sometimes come off a bit raw, there was no denying the guy's charisma. Through the hard Jersey accent emerged a blend of teddy bear and thug - and someone who seemed like a lot of fun.

But at the moment he was a stranger - and I wasn't in a gambling mood. So yeah, I lied to Tweety on the first day I met him. I guess that's kind of fucked up, but we're still friends so who cares?

Fall came soon enough, and it was suddenly time to go live the dream... by moving into a Rutgers dorm room. I was assigned to the first floor of Tinsley Hall, right in the middle of the College Avenue campus. Move-in day was, predictably, a stampede of wide-eyed college freshmen, and the energy pervading the campus was hard to avoid. It was fun, and I was excited - even if I acted cynical.

I had just arrived and was unloading stuff from my parents' car when Tweety appeared from the entrance of Tinsley Hall. As it turned out, he'd be living three floors above me. I was stoked. Although I'd ducked the chance to be his roommate, I was definitely interested in making punk rock friends at college – especially ones that happened to live so close by. Later that day Tweety would introduce me to Crawford, yet another 4th floor punk rocker, who wore an All t-shirt and immediately asked if I liked The Minutemen. The three of us would eventually become like brothers.

But at the moment, everything was new and there was much to do. I unpacked and met my roommate, who was this square dude named Ken. Ken eventually became an accountant or a claims adjuster or something along those lines, and I can say for sure that he chose the right line of work - because even at 18, the kid came off like an accountant. But he was a good roommate. Plus he went home every weekend. Score.

After making nice with Ken and throwing all my stuff onto the floor, I was off. Eager to explore and discover my new home, I decided to walk to the College Avenue Student Center, conveniently located right across the street from Tinsley Hall. The plan was to get an iced tea, smoke a cigarette, and assess the situation. Crucial stuff.

And yet what happened within my first few steps across the streets of New Brunswick couldn't have been more perfect or poetic – then, or now. As I strode toward the entrance to the Student Center, I was stopped in my tracks by a tall, lean figure. He pointed at my Operation Ivy shirt, bent toward me, and in a rich voice asked: "Do you like ska?" His name was Quincy, and he gave me a flyer for a show – his band, Inspecter 7, was playing later that week. I thanked him and tried to contain myself.

I went to the show, of course, which was at the token college-town coffee shop, Café Newz. It was a small setting, and Inspecter 7 had like eight hundred people in the band, and I liked ska enough to have a good time. And while I was there I got another flyer for another show. This Skinhead dude named Pedro gave it to me.

"Old Man" Pedro Serrano, as I came to know him, grew up in the Columbus Homes housing projects of Newark during the 1960s. He'd had it rough from the start. One of his earliest memories, for example, is of his brother being born in the middle of the 1967 Newark riots. And then there was that whole thing about being a poor, gay, Latino dude who liked punk rock. Pedro was no joke.

Bred from this tumultuous childhood, Pedro emerged to cut a striking adult figure. To me, he was the destruction of social stereotypes, embodied; an individual whose sheer existence served to challenge convention and conformity. In his own words: New Brunswick's resident, militant, homosexual Puerto Rican Skinhead.

See, when I was 18, my perceptions of the adult world made getting older a discouraging proposition. The promises of "growing up" seemed like a swirling smokescreen, deftly obscuring a reality full of corruption, subjugation, and injustice. The loss of wonder and subsequent transition to the next phase were like the grayest, most morbid funeral - layers of innocence peel away as the shelter of youth disintegrates, exposing the human creature to all the dangers of becoming another disconnected, disoriented pod person. To me, this was a fate worse than death.

There just seemed to be so little purpose in the lives of many of the adults I knew; so little meaning in how they chose to spend their time on Earth. And my encounter with punk rock had become the most life-affirming connection I'd ever experienced. I'd been to synagogue, I'd tried to like baseball, video games were ok, and comic books were definitely awesome. But punk rock spoke directly to the way I saw the world and my own everyday life. And since self-expression and staying young at heart were so important to me, music and community became my personal definition of finding "success." Dudes in suits and politicians just didn't make sense to my 18 year-old brain. All I wanted to do was be awesome.

As teenagers, Chad and I would argue over what it meant to grow up. For years, he was obsessed with the story of Peter Pan and the Lost Boys, often noting how much he loved the idea of being a kid forever. I didn't feel the same way – on the contrary, I couldn't wait to grow up, move out, and explore the world. I drew a distinction between being an "adult" and being a "grown-up". To me, adulthood meant taking ownership over one's actions – in other words, being a responsible human being. That was something I really wanted to do. But a "grown-up" – well, that was one of those withered, uninspired, uninterested and uninteresting people we'd see every day, plodding through life in our particular community. Yes, the grass was green and the pep rallies were well-attended - but the apathy on the faces of so many older people was undeniable. Some of these husks were teachers. Some of them were our friends' parents. Some of them were recent high school graduates, living at home and working as waiters. They came in all shapes and sizes, and they all sucked. The lesson was clear: if you get lazy, growing up might crush your spirit.

So as far as adults went, Pedro was compelling; walking, talking proof that punk rock didn't have to be a silly phase one passed through on the way to "adulthood." Perhaps also proof that I'd caught a little bit of Chad's Peter Pan Syndrome. After all, punk rock was for "the kids," wasn't it?

I'd always known that staying "true" as an adult might mean becoming marginalized by the greater society in one way or another – and that really worried me. Would I really have to sacrifice *so* much if I wanted to be a punk rocker for the rest of my life? Of course, I never would have admitted that I was worried about this ethical and material dilemma; instead, I might have espoused my tentative plans to smash the state or start an anarchist commune. Bullshit like that helped me dodge what seemed like an inevitable truth: one day the party would end, and I'd have to sacrifice my ideals. Ah, the logic of 18-year-olds.

But I loved my sense of individuality, and of urgency. I loved thinking for myself, and being a champion of progress and creativity. The idea that one day these values might no longer fit into my life drove me positively crazy. The music, the fanzines, the shows and the people – I loved it all so much, and the idea of losing that part of my life was simply dreadful.

So as I grew to know him, Pedro gave me hope - this fully grown man, living his adult life submerged in something often perceived by the mainstream to be "for kids," inspired me just by existing. And as I watched adulthood slowly strip the passion from young people all around me, Pedro became an anti-role model of sorts. He was sharply intelligent, unafraid, and loaded to the brim with things that might make people feel uncomfortable - for all the right reasons. Yet he always exuded positivity and peace. Amidst the then-subsiding but still common violence of the New

Jersey Skinhead scene, he was both a peacemaker and quick on his feet – which made him a real asset when problems arose.

I'd discover all of this in time, but at the moment I was glad to take a flyer for a show from just about anyone – even a weird old Skinhead. And the show sounded awesome: New Brunswick favorites The Bouncing Souls, Long Island's Mind Over Matter, and 2.5 Children, from Pennsylvania – all playing in the basement of the house at 67 Handy Street.

Handy Street sits on the outskirts of the Cook/Douglass campus of Rutgers, about two miles from my College Avenue home. And although it would have been easy to take the free university bus, I blankly decided to walk to the show. A red-headed kid named Joe who lived in the dorm room next to mine asked to tag along, so the two of us set out on a sunny Sunday afternoon to discover the charms of New Brunswick. And while I was aware that George Street – the only route I knew to take – had a ¾ mile strip with a really bad reputation, I didn't really anticipate its bountiful sketchiness.

Once we passed the fountain, however, the picture became clear.

Leaving the College Avenue campus via George Street, it's only a few blocks before you hit that famous fountain on the corner of Livingston Avenue. At the time, this intersection was the unofficial entrance to the ghetto – and walking past the fountain was not widely recommended. Once you hit the C-Town supermarket, you were officially *way* off campus.

A bit past C-Town was Remsen Avenue - the ultimate town-gown killer, with its ample drug trade, violence, and other assorted charms. Down one block further was the first of two 'Picken Chicken' restaurants, situated just a few feet from one another. They were commonly called "the red Picken Chicken" and "the blue Picken Chicken" – a distinction based on the color of the stores' respective signs. The red one sold chicken, and the blue one sold crack. Or maybe it was the other way around. Either way, we had two of them.

And then just a few blocks past the Picken Chickens began the Douglass Campus – still kind of creepy in its own unique way, but safer than the desperate war zone at its doorstep. (George Street is far less troubled today than it was in 1994. Where housing projects once stood, luxury condos are now found. You do the math.)

Anyway, Joe and I got to the show without incident. That's not to say I wasn't intimidated by my introduction to the *other* New Brunswick – I definitely was. But my agenda took precedence over any obstacles or risks I encountered. I was at my first real New Brunswick basement show - and I had a messenger bag full of zines.

The house itself was large but modest, and between (or during) bands, the 30 or 40 people there would mill about the kitchen or out front, being punk rock and cynical.

The bands played – I got to see the Bouncing Souls for the first time and Pedro did some spoken word. And in my head I was about to put myself out there, in front of a bunch of strangers, in a big way. I was hesitant, but determined. My green canvas military bag, covered in punk rock patches and buttons, had been my mother's when she was in the Israeli army. When she was 19 years old, the bag carried military supplies, rations, and a small bible. But now *I* was 19 years old. The bag was stuffed with copies of *Aneurysm*, and I was determined to empty it by the end of the show. And that's exactly what I did.

Between bands, I'd circulate amongst the small crowd. Slightly hesitant, and careful not to interrupt anyone's conversation, I did my best to sense people who would be receptive. Once I had a possible reader identified, I'd approach them and extend my hand, holding a copy of *Aneurysm*. Then came my magic question: "Hey, wanna check out a zine?"

In many ways, *Aneurysm* was my ambassador. I could use it to engage people I thought might share my interests. I didn't need small talk or dashing good looks. Instead, I offered my ideas and creative output to strangers and hoped they didn't think I was a loser. In the process, I hoped to make friends, and find what I imagined to be my people.

For me, it was day one – a new town, a scene which I'd romanticized, and the kids who comprised it. And while I was definitely self-conscious, I was also confident. I believed that punk and hardcore meant, at least in part, that people should do what they want to do, and that I didn't have to care about what others thought or said. I also believed in the power of this special kind of music – that it could bring individuals together, and break down walls of social convention. I was putting all of that into action for myself, and banking on a positive outcome; or at the very least, that the kids in New Brunswick didn't think I was a douche bag.

From that day on, I was a zine machine. With a much larger pool of potential readers than I'd ever considered, approaching strangers and trying to sell them zines became a part-time job. The worst someone could do was say "no," and sometimes that did happen. Over the years that would follow, people were generally nice enough to at least humor me – maybe they'd even go so far as to thumb through a copy and politely hand it back. But ultimately, almost everyone I approached eventually bought a copy. Maybe it was the cut of my jib, or maybe people felt bad for me, or maybe it was that I offered lots to read for a measly buck, but this was how I met countless friends – and built a decent readership along the way.

That first Handy Street show gave me a crucial shot of confidence. And of course while I was there I got more flyers for more shows. The challenge was being laid before me, and I was more than eager. Before I knew it, I was going to as many shows as possible – meeting new faces, and looking for readers. I sold zines between sets from Human Remains and Deadguy at the Cook College Café. I sold zines at a show featuring Weston and Plow United there, too. I sold zines at Middlesex County College, and at the Down Under when Lifetime played, and when Ray Cappo did spoken word. I sold zines in Philly at the Trocadero, The First Unitarian Church, JC Dobbs, the community center on 4th and Lombard and at Stalag 13. I sold them in New York City, at CBGB and ABC No Rio; at Coney Island High, The Continental and the Wetlands. From basements to night clubs to fire halls and back yards, I was there. With each new issue, I added more pages, more content, and more focus.

Things were moving.

Prior to arriving in New Brunswick, I'd called the school's newspaper to inquire about writing opportunities; specifically, ones involving music. *The Daily Targum* was pretty impressive for a college newspaper. It had a huge readership of 40,000 and was totally independent from the university, freeing it from the kinds of censorship imposed on many college publications. Not to mention that it was a *daily* newspaper, requiring its operation to be extremely "realistic." Having picked up a considerable amount of steam with *Aneurysm* by this point, I was hungry to extend myself further; to grow as a writer, and to reach more people. And not long after school started, I got a call from someone at the *Targum*, asking if I wanted to come in and talk about writing. My media obsession pulsed, like a rip in the space-time continuum.

The music editor was an indie-rock guy named Brandon, and we had some things in common. He, too, published a fanzine (called *White Bread*). We also shared a certain sensibility about our respective writing styles, despite glaring differences in musical taste and opinion. But perhaps the most obvious similarity we shared was our demographic – we were both white boys from South Jersey who liked independent rock music.

I'd only written a couple of record reviews by the time Brandon sent me on my first real assignment. Biohazard, House of Pain, and a then-unknown band called Korn were booked by the Rutgers Program Council to play the College Avenue Gym – essentially, right across the street from my dorm. It was my first feature article, and I was psyched.

Everything was up to me. Doors were scheduled to open at 7 p.m., so I got to the gym at 2 p.m. I was hoping that, just by hanging around, I'd stumble across someone from one of the bands, and snag an interview.

And whether it was my early-bird ethic or just dumb luck, I hit the jackpot almost immediately. As I stood in the empty gym soon after my arrival, who should walk through the door other than Biohazard bassist and arguable front-man Evan Seinfeld, bouncing a basketball? I approached him and introduced myself, asking if someone from the band was available to answer a couple of quick questions. Evan passed me over to guitarist and vocalist Billy Graziadei, who politely responded to my boring questions with short, no-nonsense answers. As the interview wrapped up, Evan walked up and asked me if I wanted to play a game of basketball with him and Billy, against the guys from House of Pain. And though only aware of the sport's most fundamental aspects, I nearly threw up in my mouth to say, "Yes, Biohazard. I would very much like to play basketball with you against House of Pain." As if on cue, Everlast, DJ Lethal and Danny Boy all appeared, and all of a sudden I found myself in a game of pickup. But knowing that the longer I stayed in the game the greater chance I had of looking stupid, I excused myself almost immediately.

Now by this point, punk rock had all but destroyed any illusions I had built up in my head about the concept of celebrity. My days were, in fact, supposed to be based on a foundation of humanistic reality – that is, that all people are the same, and that any differences we can observe are ones created solely by history, circumstance, and the limits of our collective and individual intelligence.

But I couldn't help being psyched. If I could just show up, hoping to talk to a band and wind up playing basketball with them against *another* band, anything could happen. Insert something about the possibilities seeming limitless, and it's enough to make any teenager's head spin.

I went to the show later that evening, wrote the piece, and it came out fine. Overall, it was unremarkable, except for a condescending rant about Korn and how much I hated them. And while I can't say that my opinion on the band has changed much over the past 10 years, I'll admit that I didn't have to go as negative as I did. Especially since this story ends with Korn threatening me. It turns out they had a friend from Rutgers who'd shown them the article. This friend, who also happened to write for the *Targum*, then relayed a message to me from Korn, saying that I should "watch my back" whenever they came to town. Of course, I was already one step ahead of them, having sworn to stay as far as possible from them and their music.

One thing I really liked about Crawford and Tweety was that they were both creative people who, like me, used media as a form of expression. Crawford, for example, was a fountain of frenetic, creative energy. He played bass, was into sketch comedy, and could talk with both wit and wisdom about books, films, and other cultural offerings. Crawford also had a fanzine, called *Tear Down Babylon*; it consisted almost entirely of collage, and was an intense mixture of social commentary, absurdist humor, and grim personal reflection. Crawford's zine had a rich, artful design that was a far cry from the slop-inspired stylistics I'd given *Aneurysm*.

Crawford, Tweety and I even wound up producing a zine together. Aptly named *Bored College Punks*, it came together spontaneously one night out of – go figure - boredom. *BCP* lasted a surprising two issues, both of which consisted of two double-sided photocopies stapled once in the corner - high school vocabulary test style, not unlike the earliest issues of *Aneurysm*.

But Tweety's real calling wasn't fanzines. It was radio.

For years, a guy named Mat Gard had hosted a weekly punk radio show called *Radio Riot* on WRSU, the Rutgers radio station. Over time, the show had become something of an institution, as did its legendary zine counterpart. *Radio Riot,* the fanzine, was nothing more than a single piece of 8.5"x11" letter paper, but Mat had been putting it out for years to both fan and critical acclaim. Even when I was in high school, I'd read gushing reviews of *Radio Riot* in zines like *Maximum RockandRoll* and *HeartattaCk*.

But that fall, Mat Gard had decided that it was time to move on. With a time slot to bestow, he wanted a replacement who would somehow continue the spirit of the show; apparently, Tweety was the man. And while they were considerable shoes to fill, Tweety stepped up to the occasion with more than enough talent and charisma to get the job done. Just like that, *Radio Riot* became *Verbal Assault*, and Tweety became a DJ. He was a natural when it came to projecting personality over the airwaves; he also had a good sense of how to keep the show new and interesting from week to week. Plus, Tweety had a ton of records and knew a lot about them. For the next couple of years, he'd lug that vinyl up those stairs to WRSU's studio, next door to the Targum offices. Each week, Tweety would spin records and take requests, announce upcoming shows and have guests from bands drop in to chat. Crawford and I were often there, too, as were plenty of other people. Sometimes one of us would go on the air with Tweety, but usually we just yelled dumb shit from the back of the room. It didn't take long before the radio station was a weekly ritual.

Those first few months set the tone for the rest of the year. Tweety and Crawford and I would become super tight. And our friendship – arguably, almost our entire lives – revolved around music; how it made us feel, and how it inspired is. While our tastes and opinions were quite varied, we were nonetheless bound strongly together. It wasn't necessarily *what* we were that drew us together – it was how.

And hey, college was good for learning stuff, too! Placed into my very first Political Science class at Rutgers as a second choice, I wound up falling in love with the subject. Studying the causes of war, how international trade works and all that stuff? Well it was right up my alley. The world was fucked, and this was something that my friends and I seemed to know almost instinctively; and knowing more details only served as more ammo for the war in my head.

In May, Brandon (the music editor at *Targum*) graduated – and I got his job. Which was, of course, good news. In fact, the goodness seemed to be just about everywhere – people, bands, music – my scheme of moving to New Brunswick had worked in spades, and I was straight-up titillated. There was only one piece of bad news - the school year was over, and I had to go back to my parents' house.

That summer, I broke up with Marlton, NJ. Really, it was something of a blur. There was just so much I was missing from my new life back in New Brunswick – namely, like, everything. But with nowhere to live in town that summer, I had no other choice. So to make the most out of the situation I decided that when I wasn't working my stupid summer deli job, I would rock the fuck out. If the summer of '95 was about anything at all, it was The Lost Boys.

With three months ahead of us, Chad and I decided to start a band that would break up when school resumed. The idea was to write and record a minimum of four songs, and play at least one show – all before the end of summer. We'd practice in Chad's sun room. He'd been playing guitar for a few years and would therefore be the main axe-wielder. Since I'd sung for a couple of terrible bands in high school, I would be the front man.

To round out the lineup, we enlisted our good friends Tim and John. They'd been playing music together for years, and they were awesome; well-trained, and way better than us. Plus, they were kind of getting into punk rock. So when, in the spirit of fun, they agreed to take part – well it was cool news. Not only did we have a lineup, but some of us actually had experience playing music; it made us an official band. Taking our name from Chad's then-burgeoning Peter Pan obsession, we became The Lost Boys. And we would be *terrible*.

Tim, you see, was a guitar player. But we already had one of those. So Tim became our drummer – the only reason for this being that he had a drum set, which he did not know from his ass.

Make no mistake; we all tried our hardest – especially Chad and I. Even if the collective effort fell short of even being *passable*, we wanted to do the best we could. These were, after all, songs Chad and I had actually written, and like most things we did back then we tried our best to pour our hearts out.

But Tim was so fucking bad. *So* bad.

Still, we worked hard; despite the absurd timetable and absurd drumming, we recorded a four-song demo: the ultra-limited (thank God) *Firestorm to Pasteurize* cassette; and played not one, but *two* shows. The first was the backyard of a house in Marlton, at a high school pool party/barbeque. It wasn't a "real" show, of course, which was good - because we weren't a real band.

Still, playing music (no matter how badly) was a great way to pass the time; and between that and slicing deli meat, my time away from New Brunswick seemed to rocket by. And by August we'd all but buried The Lost Boys – until I got a phone call from Tweety. Earlier that summer he and I had spoken on the phone, and I'd mentioned my summertime rock experiment; now he was calling me at my parents' house to see if we wanted to play a show with Heidnik Stew and some other bands at a coffee shop in South Jersey.

Whoa.

Excited and slightly stunned, I called the other Lost Boys to see if they could do it. This was a real show and we, after all, were not actually a real band. So the idea of someone calling and wanting us to play was unexpected, and sort of hilarious. Although I do recall that Tim was hesitant – and understandably so - we wound up saying yes.

Other than Heidnik Stew, the lineup included a bunch of familiar bands from the Central Jersey punk scene, most of which I knew because Heidnik Stew had played with them in the past: Shower With Goats, Boxcar, and a band called The Missing Children. And now on the bill – The Lost Boys!

Really, though – Tim was terrible.

But we played anyway, and it was a whole lot of fun. More than anything, I was honored and gratified by my friends, and their awesome offer to let me participate. Asking to play a "real" show with The Lost Boys was not something I'd even considered, because as far as bands go, we weren't very good. In reality, I had to overcome my own insecurities, and trust in what I already knew: that bands weren't just about how well people could play their instruments, how many fans they had, or how much merch they sold. There was one characteristic that seemed to trump all of those values, and it was as simple as one word – heart. You didn't have to be a prodigy, messiah, or pinup. You just had to play, and mean it. And if there was any shred of falseness to be found – well, it seemed like most of the punk kids I knew could tell. There was very little room for bullshit bands. So we might have sucked, but we meant it one hundred percent.

Of course, I don't imagine that any of us thought about that show exactly in those terms. If nothing else, it was a fun way to end the summer. So The Lost Boys called it a day. Chad headed off to Washington, D.C. for his first year at American University, and soon enough I would be back in New Brunswick, reunited with my new friends and eager to get something going. Whatever it was.

Three – 1995-1996: Frelinghuysen Hall

Square dude Ken and I had gotten along well as roommates during the previous year and decided that if it wasn't broke we needn't fix it; in the fall of '95 we were assigned to a room on the second floor of Frelinghuysen Hall - one of three "river dorms" tucked in at the back end of College Avenue. Frelinghuysen had kooky nicknames like "Freezing-huysen" and was (and still is to my knowledge) the epitome of a cold, crappy dorm.

Crawford had transferred into Demarest Hall, which was the "special" dorm for "creative" types. Most of your serious drama nerds, for example, wound up there. Lots of Wiccans, and smelly people, and crazies. No shortage of *Monty Python*, if you know what I mean.

As for Tweety – well, he moved into an off-campus apartment at 220 Hamilton Street. It was a dump, and perfectly suited for the chaos that would erupt there every twenty minutes or so over the next year. He'd recently shed his voluminous hair and Tweety Bird suspenders, transforming completely into a Skinhead. I was thrown off when I first saw the "new" Tweety, but the change made sense and suited him well. And perhaps in celebration of his newfound direction in life, Tweety seemed to be always playing host in his new pad - which usually involved lots of Skinheads, drinking malt liquor. I wonder how his roommates felt about that.

67 Handy Street was kicking off the new school year with a Sunday Matinee, and I was psyched. In addition to local posi hero dudes Strength 691, I was *finally* going to see Farside, from California. I was a huge fan at the time, and they rarely toured. But by the time I got to the show, Farside had already played and left, having to catch their flight back to the West Coast. It may have been the only New Brunswick hardcore show to start on time. I was bummed, and decided to leave after Strength 691 finished playing.

At the bus stop, I ran into Zak, a red-haired freshman who had moved into Demarest Hall. I'd seen his naturally orange mohawk in the first days of the school year and had introduced myself, so we knew each other, but only slightly. Zak was waiting for the bus with another kid, his roommate, Fleming. Fleming seemed like a metal kid, with long black hair and the kind of sleek, modern sunglasses that make a person look like an insect. I got a sketchy vibe from him; maybe it was because he didn't want to buy a fanzine.

Zak and Fleming were the first of many new people I would meet – lots of them. Like the kids who lived in Clothier Hall.

There was the acerbic, hilarious kid with a purple mohawk, who introduced himself as Fid Vicious, Slayer of Bitches. Fid played guitar (though at the time, barely) in a band called Degradation, back home in Allentown, NJ. Jaime was another Clothier resident, and played drums in a band called instil; he and Fid already knew each other from shows their bands had played together in high school. There was this weird kid named Pedro, but we already had a Pedro, and so he soon became known as Little Pedro (and later, Silky). Christine was a saucy little punk rock chick from Staten Island, and we wound up dating for a little while, until I cheated on her. There was a kid named Joe Crucified, because he was straight edge. And Sue was a red-headed girl who played guitar and liked to shoplift.

Now don't get me wrong – I'd never once felt at a loss for friends since I'd first come to New Brunswick. But eventually, most people went home, because they didn't live on College Avenue. There were exceptions, like Matt H. (who had an awesome band called The Immaculate Abortion) and Jay S. (who had an awesome band called Automaton). But as cool as those dudes might have been, they just weren't my close friends. Especially in the beginning, most late nights consisted of just me, Crawford, and Tweety.

Which by no means was a bad thing. On the contrary, the three of us became family over that year, and I doubt any one of us would have had it any other way.

But all these new personalities really added something, at least for me. I wanted that diverse, creative group. Sure, nay-sayers might question the diversity in a group of young Americans who liked punk rock. But there was a strong spirit there; a reverence for self-expression, delivered with industrious creativity. Some of us saw potential for social activism or cultural solidarity; other people saw fun and companionship. And some people just wanted to drink. But for each in their own way, it was something of an "us against the world" situation. And we were way into group-commiseration.

One night I was at the Douglass Student Center to see Weston play. It was a night as good as any other; I'd get to see a band I liked, and maybe sell a couple of zines.

I spent most of the show minding my own business when two punky-looking dudes approached me and asked if I played guitar. Well, I *had* a guitar. I had a couple, actually. And I could play them, sort of. Or rather, I knew some chords. I could pick out some… rhythms? So I said "Yes, I play guitar," but with the caveat that I wasn't very good. It was the understatement of the eon.

They introduced themselves to me as Scott and Dave, and assured me that my minimal musical ability would be sufficient. Their band was, after all, called Worthless – and as far as the dudes seemed to be concerned, I *looked* cool enough to join. We exchanged phone numbers and they gave me their demo. We got along well, and Scott and Dave seemed like good dudes, so I was understandably stoked. Except for the guitar thing.

The first thing I did when I got home that night was to listen to Worthless' demo. I liked what I heard – fun, sloppy punk with ska parts; like a crappy version of Operation Ivy. And to compliment the band's... lack of musical pretense... they had classically adolescent song titles like "Five Dollar Donut," "Pink Bananas," and "Fat Albert."

As far as taste and style went (or lack thereof), it seemed to be a match for me. So a few days later, Scott and Dave visited Frelinghuysen Hall to teach me some songs. My guess is that from the first note I played, the jig was up. I mean, Worthless' songs were as simple as could be, but I could barely make it through any of them. Officially a shitty guitar player, my turn as a member of Worthless ended there and then, without so much as one real practice. Still, I doubt any of us would have considered my audition a waste of time – because as friends, we got along great. And I'd wind up going to a *lot* of Worthless shows in the future.

Worthless shows were kind of like a train wreck. As their lineup was constantly revolving, it always seemed that someone in the band had just joined and hadn't quite yet mastered the songs. Not that it mattered, of course, because everyone in the band was concentrating almost exclusively on being visually absurd. Whether they were wearing one of their various masks or running around like idiots, Worthless had made a habit of making up for slop with pure spectacle.

If Worthless the band was sort of goofy, it's because the people *in* the band were totally insane, with Scott and Dave at the helm. Like many young people, they had developed a complex and specific comedy culture among their circle of friends. And it was effortless. Scott and Dave didn't have to try to be quirky, clever weirdos; they *were* quirky, clever weirdos. Scott, for example, decorated his dorm room by stapling men's briefs to the wall. He once went through a phase where he wouldn't drink anything that wasn't blue. And Scott occasionally wore a mask that transformed him into the infamous "Oscar", an alter ego whose existence seemed to be based solely around the idea of making people really uncomfortable and/or confused. And so birds of a feather, et cetera, and all of a sudden you have a band and their little posse, and everyone is a little bit of a kook.

Throughout my first year in New Brunswick, the Down Under had always been there. From Frodus and Kurbjaw to 4 Walls Falling and Standpoint, this club in the basement of the Livingston Hotel had been a crucial fixture for punk and hardcore music in New Brunswick. So when the Down Under did its last show over the summer of '95, it was definitely a loss. But for the kids in Clothier Hall, none of that seemed to have anything to do with anything. They were already moving forward.

On December 3, 1995 a number of Clothier punk rock-type people with their own bands conspired - through the magic of student government - to take over their building's lounge for a few hours with a punk rock show.

A band called The Steadfasts played first. They were a new band that Zak had put together with Sue. Frizzy mohawk and all, Zak turned out to be a pretty good band guy – maybe more so than I'd anticipated. So as far as openers go, they definitely could have been much worse. I don't remember a single one of The

Steadfasts' poppy punk songs, but can comfortably testify that they weren't garbage. Degradation played next. Like Fid, they were fun, punchy, deliberately adolescent and habitually self-deprecating. And although Fid was always saying how terrible a band Degradation was, his claims seemed to be overblown. Mostly.

Of course, being a little sloppy and a little silly was okay by me – to the point that if a band had worn lobster costumes and played balalaikas, I would have eaten it up. I probably still would. I was into anything – ANYTHING – that smashed "establishment" models of what it meant to be a rock band. So it was completely justified for me to love bands that sucked. To this day, I maintain the right to invoke this reasoning when discussing music with friends or family. Don't fuck with me.

The bottom line was that, to me, being a good musician or writing good songs had nothing to do with being in a band that mattered. On the contrary, musicianship that was *too* skilled always ran the ideological risk of being masturbatory, bullshit rock star stuff. I loved the populism and democracy I saw in the act of letting anyone with enough guts go up there and rock out.

That's probably why I had such mixed feelings about the last band to play: instil. Now at the time, I perceived most straightedge kids as being at least a little bit pretentious, no matter how cool or nice they were otherwise. It certainly wasn't the straight-edge lifestyle or values that I found to be offensive; it was the proselytizing. Perhaps un-ironically, a synonym for "proselytize" is "instil." You get the picture.

But instil weren't just edge, or vegan. They fucking *cried* at their shows. In screamy, rhythmic, deeply personal songs about tragic human experiences, they appeared to chase some sort of emotional catharsis, as if the five of them collectively desired to become an exposed nerve ending, disguised as a band. Some fans – obviously already familiar with the band – shared in the experience. To me, it smacked of bullshit.

And yet, there were some things about instil that I couldn't ignore. Musically, for example, they were fucking awesome. Tight, aggressive, abrasive, and inherently defiant in their own way. They had that special energy; maybe you know the one I mean. And as far as people – well, instil were cool dudes.

Was their display of emotion that night fabricated? Possibly – but it doesn't really matter. What *isn't* fabricated these days? Governments, opinions, value systems, curricula – we have been bootlegging things on a mind-boggling scale for thousands of years. And did you know that laughter therapy is widely accepted in the medical community as being able to help relieve stress, combat disease, and strengthen the immune system? Fuckin' medical facts, bro. So even if the dudes in instil were fake-crying – and I don't think they were – who cares? Who can say that making oneself cry is any less beneficial to the human experience than crying involuntarily when upset?

Still, one thing gnawed at me - what about fun? To me, instil didn't look like they were having fun when they played, *at all*. On the contrary, everything seemed to be about pain, and it showed. Band members collapsed to the ground mid-song; audience members sobbed; it was very powerful, and/or very weird. But definitely not fun.

Regardless, I got over it. It was hard to hate a band made up of such nice dudes who could kick O.G. screamo ass.

There weren't a bazillon people there, and the bands that played never really made the big time, but in my heart that first Clothier show will always be monumental. Maybe it was the chemicals that go off in the brains of people at 19 years old – the ones that make you want to be on the team, or in the frat, or in the club – but I felt so excited, and at home.

It was a Friday night in December and I was in my dorm room when the phone rang. I answered, and a strained male voice on the line asked for me by name. "Let me speak to Ronen, the blue-haired goon." Clearly, I was the target of a prank call. I figured that the caller was one of my friends, having some fun and meaning no offense. Having made plenty of prank calls of my own by that age, I was ready to take it with a grain of salt. I'd be a sport.

But almost immediately, the prank began to feel unfriendly. The prankster and a sidekick became flatly antagonistic, digging increasingly deeper in their effort to provoke an angry reaction from me. Unfortunately for them, this wasn't the type of thing to upset me, so I just kind of went with it. This frustrated the merry pranksters, who then grew even more determined to get my proverbial goat.

And then came the spark: it was revealed that the prank call was being broadcast live on on WRSU, the Rutgers University radio station.

Admittedly, my goat was now gotten, and I finally hung up the telephone. Two or three more prank calls came through before I decided enough was enough; at the very, least I needed to know who was behind it all. Since Tweety was a DJ at the station, I figured he would know the on-air schedule. I called him and asked who had a show on WRSU at that moment.

"Why?" he asked, his speech slightly slurred.

"Someone's fucking with me on the air."

"I'll call you right back," he said. Click.

A minute later, my phone rang again. This time, it wasn't my prankster calling – it was Tweety. "We'll be right over. Wait outside."

It wasn't what I expected to hear - and I wasn't sure what

exactly Tweety meant by "we," but I began to assume it was the battalion of drunken Skinheads I'd heard readying for battle in the background when he called me back. It turns out that I had given them a reason to live that evening. The night was young, they'd been drinking for long enough, and now it was time to defend my honor. Or something.

I threw on shoes and a jacket and went down to wait on George Street. It was only a couple of minutes before two carloads of stinking drunk Skinheads – plus Fid and a truly lovely and intimidating Skinhead girl named Christina - peeled around the corner and came to an abrupt stop. "Get in," yelled Tweety from the passenger seat of one of the cars. I followed the instruction.

Now up to this point, Tweety and I had collectively spoken roughly 25 words on the issue of these prank calls; and not being a fighter, violent conflict wasn't necessarily the solution I would have suggested. But this was now happening with or without me, so I figured that maybe I should go. At the very least, maybe I'd be able to do some damage control and minimize the chaos that seemed imminent. I knew I could count on Fid to do the same.

As we peeled down George Street, Tweety explained that he'd called the radio station and gotten similar treatment as I had. From the moment his call had been answered, Tweety could tell that he was not speaking to official station personnel. He bristled, asking, "Who *is* this?" Well that's when the whole thing went to shit, and the prankster, careless in his prankitude, made his critical error. Unaware of Tweety's size, power, or apparent thirst for street justice, the person on the phone replied sarcastically, "Who is *this*?," followed by some curse words. Oopsy.

That mistake mixed with malt liquor to seal the deal, and Tweety delivered the subpoena: "I'm your worst nightmare." And while in most cases a statement like that might be a tad melodramatic, this time it was pretty much true. I suppose that all of this helped me feel a little less guilty for these unassuming pranksters possibly getting the shit kicked out of them. At least now they had not only targeted me; they'd also taunted my hot-headed friend, and his crew of scary, drunk, bald-headed people. As both cars tore around corners on the short drive to WRSU, we listened to the radio. The merry pranksters continued to whoop it up about me and their "worst nightmare," never thinking that one of us might have a key to the radio station; or that we would be dropping by momentarily. They dug their graves deeper with each smug chuckle.

In reality, I was worried about whomever we found behind the microphone. They clearly hadn't anticipated a fistfight when they decided to pull a prank on me and broadcast it. And I definitely didn't want anyone to get hurt. Yet it was nice to have backup from such a robust and *enthusiastic* support network, even if the imminent beat down would be rooted more in beer and boredom than a deep dedication to me as an individual.

In a matter of moments we arrived at WRSU, where Tweety used his slash card and we entered the building effortlessly. Stomping loudly up the stairs to the station offices, we plowed into the main studio room and the six or seven people we found there all turned white. With the surprising exceptions of Zak and Sue, the faces in this crowd were familiar at best.

We had two questions: who had made the calls, and where were they? Everyone in the room, of course, denied having anything to do with anything. They claimed that the *real* pranksters – two fellows named Todd and Pablo - had already left the building. We later found this to be partially true. They had, in fact, heard us coming up the stairs when we first arrived, and scurried to the top of the stairwell to quietly ride out chaos. They also claimed that the whole thing had been made possible by Christine, who was also nowhere to be seen. She had been the one with my phone number - as noted earlier, Christine and I had at one point spent some time together. As also noted earlier, said romance ended when I cheated on her. Strangely, the whole thing had snowballed into this radio studio about to break out into a riot.

Drunken Skinheads backed various indie rock nerds into corners around the room as Fid and I tried our best to keep things from spinning out of control. Everyone was a potential target for reprisal - and of course, the studio was broadcasting live. Luckily, listeners heard music, and not the chaos that was taking place.

Like Tweety, for example, yelling in red-headed Sue's face. She'd been continuously and repeatedly collapsing in fear from the moment we'd barged in, and now Tweety had her cowering in a corner as he demanded that she reveal Todd and Pablo's location. Sue squirmed and denied knowing anything, and Tweety's tone grew more menacing. "Tell me!" he barked with authority, visibly piercing Sue's personal comfort zone with both voice and physical proximity.

Finally, Tweety backed off a little bit, yelling, "You're lucky you're a bitch, so I won't hit you." He paused, and then completed his thought. "Christina! Come over here and hit this bitch!"

Then Tweety moved onto Zak.

It sucked to see Zak there, because I had been under the impression that we were friends. But now, more than anything, I feared for his safety. And so did he. His approach was to just sit there, very still, on a stool by the turntables, and deny any involvement. Zak's denial was bullshit, of course, because he'd been the one who'd answered the phone when Tweety called. But he sat there and smiled nervously, trying to look calm as the Skinheads stumbled around the room looking for nerds to pummel. It may have been an attempt to say, "Hey, dudes, I'm not nervous!" But my research confirms that the kid was pooping his mental pants.

Putting his face up to Zak's, Tweety commanded, "You have ten seconds to tell me where they are!" There was a momentary pause, and then Tweety began counting. For whatever reason, he only got to "two" before clocking Zak in the head. Tweety once again yelled, "Tell me where they are!" Zak just sat there, reeling from the strike and stumping for his innocence. He didn't really have much choice.

Somehow that punch to the head was the worst we'd see that night. With it clear that the actual pranksters had really fled the scene, the situation seemed to diffuse. The Skinheads were convinced to leave the station and once we got outside I went home. But Tweety, with a couple of his most trusted, most dangerous homies, decided that the night was not over. They wanted Todd and Pablo.

Which brings us to Zak in his underwear.

Zak was freaking the fuck out. Afraid that his encounter with Skinhead justice wasn't quite over, he rushed home to Demarest Hall and tore all indications of punk rock residence off of his dorm room door. Killing the lights and getting into bed, he hoped for a good night's sleep.

But just as soon as he'd gone into hiding, the game was on again. As Zak and Fleming lay silently in the dark, three angry Skinheads could be heard lumbering through the hallway, mumbling things like "Which door is his?" With a tiny breath, Zak turned to Fleming and whispered famously, "You don't think they'll hit a guy in his underwear, do you?"

But with no Misfits posters on the door, there was simply no way that Tweety and his boys could know which door to knock down. Within a few moments the Skins seemed to give up and the hallway became silent. And then, just as Zak began to think that he'd dodged a bullet, there came a sudden pounding on his door. A gruff voice called from the other side, and it was Tweety's – he was back once again, and somehow he'd figured out which door was Zak's.

Tweety had already punched him in the head that evening, and now he'd come calling with two of his scariest pals. For Zak, it was do or die. And so facing up to what was now unavoidable, Zak put on his pants and opened the door. And as Tweety and his pals demanded to know where Todd and Pablo had gone, Zak told the truth (and hoped for the best). He insisted that he didn't know where Todd and Pablo were, and that it was even possible they'd skipped town.

Zak must have been pretty convincing, because Tweety and pals soon gave up and left. But that one night had left enough of an impression that Zak skipped plans to attend a local show the next day for fear of encountering any associated Skinheads.

Nonetheless, things smoothed out and before long, the real-life "Radio Riot" became water under the bridge. Not only did Zak and I bury the hatchet, but within a few weeks he and Tweety were drinking together with some kids at Clothier Hall; Tweety even wound up back at Zak's room, where he finished a bottle of Jagermeister and then passed out on the floor. Unable to wake him, Zak and Fleming had no choice but to let Tweety sleep there that night. And so he did, with no blanket or pillow. Zak and Fleming didn't get much sleep that night. According to Fleming, Tweety spent the night farting and snoring "like a wounded animal."

It was an early spring show at Handy Street, and as often was the case, things had gotten off to a late start. Taking advantage of the time, I tried to sell some copies of *Aneurysm*.

"Hey, wanna check out a zine?"

Now usually, even when someone was going to buy a

copy, the initial response to my anonymous solicitation was lukewarm. But not this one particular guy at the show. He wasn't just *interested* in checking out one of my fanzines – he was psyched. It took me by surprise, and we chatted for a short while. It wasn't until later that I realized my new friend played guitar in the very band I had come to see – Lifetime. They were quickly becoming one of my favorites.

A huge part of my personal take on punk and hardcore has always been the relationship between bands and fans. Throughout high school I'd gone to plenty of concerts, but they were always *concerts*. The audience would buy tickets, show up, fill a giant room and wait for the band to make its entrance. The band would eventually emerge from an unseen, unknown realm and play their set at a safe distance from any of their fans. Bouncers would maintain order and when the performance was finished, the band would retreat back to their hidden sanctuary. The fans went home and that was that.

But *shows* were much different, and the kids knew this. In fact, one of the things that always felt most powerful to me about punk rock was the way that it is nurtured in small physical spaces. I couldn't have imagined anything more cathartic than sweating through the shitty sound systems and grimy bodies, not to mention coming face to face with the bands I loved as they played their songs. These are the kinds of events which had no outward connection to the mainstream rock concert experience; and they helped define the setting in which I felt most excited about life.

So, of course, when New Bedford Fest rolled around in March of '96, I wanted to go. Badly. But there was one small problem: I had absolutely no way to get there.

The line-up for this Massachusetts event was massive. Bands included Damnation A.D., The Enkindles, Ten Yard Fight,

Despair, Game Face and a ton of others. It was also the last show for the well-known political Canadian band Chokehold. At the time, these were some of the biggest bands in punk rock and hardcore and I'd never seen most of them.

So two days before the show, I made a last-minute resolution that it was Massachusetts or bust. Sadly, my determination didn't change reality. All of my friends' cars were full and finding a ride in time seemed unlikely.

That's when I had my bright idea. Since Lifetime was playing the fest, I'd just call Dan and ask him for a ride. Chalk it up to bravery or lack of shame, but I dialed and asked. Dan's answer was tentative; he'd have to check if there would be room in the van and get back to me. For one reason or another, I wasn't optimistic.

But the call came through the next day, with good news and one catch: Lifetime wouldn't be coming straight home after their Saturday performance. If I wanted a ride back to New Brunswick, I'd have to stay with the band overnight somewhere in Rhode Island and then drive directly to NYC the next morning for a Sunday matinee at CBGB.

Needless to say, I was eager to accommodate the conditions. Not only had I managed to get a ride to New Bedford Fest on such short notice, and not only was I going to see a ton of awesome bands, but I'd be hanging out with my hometown anti-heroes all weekend.

Of course, there were some awkward moments. As I showed up at 67 Handy Street to catch my ride on that clear Saturday morning, it dawned on me: I really didn't know any of these dudes, and we were about to spend a lot of time together. And while I was psyched to be having the experience, it wasn't effortless. Not to mention, everyone was a few years older than me. At that time in a person's life, a few years is like a lifetime - no pun intended.

Luckily, I was too excited to care. Wearing my spiky leather collar and ready to rock, I sat in silent jubilation as we pulled onto Route 18 to start our north-bound journey. There were eight of us in the van: me, the band, and that weekend's roadies - Spliedt and Joey Tea Bags. Joey didn't say much, but Spliedt and I talked quite a bit. As we rode up to MA, he folded and stapled copies of his zine, *Crash Position*. Spliedt wanted to have enough copies for the fest and I could relate. I'd come strapped with a thick stack of *Aneurysm*. Of course, we traded copies.

The ride itself was a blur. We listened to Al Green or Marvin Gaye. Some people slept. others rearranged the letters on Jade Tree Records stickers to say things like "retard" and "pee jar."

Stinky and fatigued, I was nonetheless psyched when we got to New Bedford. I was also eager to stretch my legs, and walk around. The New Bedford YMCA had been transformed into a temporary hardcore town square, and I was ready to get my social on.

Like most of the other kids there, I was stoked on the punk rock flea market that composed the "other" part of the show. Beyond the usual merch that bands were selling, there were a number of large distros with vast selections of punk and hardcore records, both new and old. Patches, buttons, zines – it could all be found here. And of course, there were tables dedicated to distributing information – human rights, animal rights and other. We might have been on the precipice of the information age, but to us everything was still mail order and paper fanzines. So having so much stuff of the DIY (Do it Yourself) variety in one place was an exciting and important opportunity to snag items you might otherwise have a difficult time finding. Not to mention the chance to meet interesting, creative, like-minded people from other parts of the country.

And then of course, there was the music itself.

The second-most memorable performance that day was from a Philly band called Switched On. They were frenetic, slamming through 25 minutes or so of fast, chaotic hardcore. But what really got my attention was how their set ended - it was something I'd never seen or even considered possible. The vocalist said that for their last song, they'd be throwing the microphone into the crowd, so that everyone could participate. He encouraged people in the crowd to express themselves; to say what they had to say.

While I know this was certainly not the first time something like this had taken place, I was breathless: the destruction of any barrier – real or imagined - between the band and their audience; the spontaneity with which the crowd helped craft the song; the power of a band being able to induce an improvised collaboration; and the implicit freedom in the act itself. It was beautiful.

For me, this was the theme of the weekend. After all, ignoring those imaginary barriers had gotten me to Massachusetts. Think about it – does Bono walk around in front of the venue before he plays a show? Does Christina Aguilera show any interest (genuine or otherwise) in the creative efforts of her fans? Could you call up Nickelback and ask them for a ride to their wack-ass concert? And would Celine Dion ever pass the microphone out into the crowd so that her fans could unite with her in the glory of artistic expression?

And would Celine Dion please shut the fuck up?

It was early evening when Lifetime got ready to play their set, and after helping the band with their equipment, Spliedt, Joey Tea Bags and I positioned ourselves on the side of the stage to watch the show. The crowd was buzzing with anticipation. Lifetime was just hitting their stride at the time, I was stoked.

The band broke open their set and kids immediately went off. They rocked, the crowd moved, and everything was great. Awesome, even. That is, until the bad thing happened.

It was a few minutes into Lifetime's set when, from the corner of my eye, I caught sight of something moving downward. And in the instant when it happened – with the band shredding and the crowd rocking out - well, there was a lot going on. So I registered the falling object in the corner of my eye as a sweater or some other object that must have been dropped accidentally from the balcony area, where many kids were watching the action.

But within a few moments of seeing and mentally filing away the falling sweater, Spliedt and I realized that something was going on in the crowd below where the mysterious falling object would have landed. A number of people were gathering around one spot and trying to make room around it. We signaled to the band that something was going wrong and that they needed to stop playing.

The falling object turned out not to be a sweater, but a person who had decided to jump from the balcony into the crowd below. As one might expect, he landed on another person, who of course was knocked to the ground, eyes rolling into the back of his head, having a seizure, et cetera.

Seeing the results of his poor choice, the jumper quickly tried to slink away from the situation. He was, of course, stopped before he could melt into the crowd. A number of individuals had spotted him and the kids refused to let him leave until everything was resolved and all responsibilities had been taken.

I'm fairly certain that the victim of the incident left the show in an ambulance, unconscious from the time he was smashed into the concrete floor. Lots of people who were there that day have confessed to me that the incident left them feeling uneasy. I myself wondered quite plainly: how could something so bad happen in the midst of something that was supposed to be so good?

At the end of the night, I piled into the van with the band and Spliedt and Joey Tea Bags, and we went to some kid's house. We slept there, on the floor, and I used my bag as a pillow because I hadn't thought of bringing one. (Needless to say, I didn't have a blanket, either.) I was in a strange place, feeling kind of weird – and there was a lot of farting.

But the next day things seemed a little less foreign. Maybe it was seeing everyone's morning faces that did the trick. Or maybe it's just because things feel less dramatic in the daylight. Either way, we were off.

Unlike the ride to New Bedford, our sprint to New York City took a little bit of patience. Hitting massive traffic coming out of New England and then, of course, coming into the city, I was learning firsthand the "hurry up and wait" reality of being in a touring band. And there was one more annoyance – I had to poop. Badly.

This, of course, is one biological need of human beings that is completely incompatible with New York City traffic. And while the reviled pee jar (or Arizona iced tea bottle) might have been there in most moments of road-warrior need, taking a shit is a completely different story. So hopefully I'll be forgiven for the mild panic that overtook me as we traversed the Cross-Bronx Expressway. I wondered silently: "Am I going to shit my pants in front of these dudes?"

But I found that peaceful place in my mind - the one that allows people to avoid the public emptying of bowels – and we made it to the venue "in time." And it was simply for the reason that I had to go *so* badly that I did what few, if any, will admit to doing, or even considering: I took a dump in the bathroom at CBGB.

To be fair, it was 1 o'clock in the afternoon, and the club was still empty. Although the matinee was scheduled to start at 3, we had gotten to CBs early enough that we were the only people there other than some bar employees. So with no better choice available, I made my move. (Pun intended.)

Walking down the stairs at the back of CBGB, the bathroom came into eyeshot almost immediately. There was no door or curtain; no privacy. And the walls, the fixtures – shit, what am I doing here? Trying to describe the bathroom at CBGB? Dude, it was the fucking bathroom at CBGB. That's enough of a description. But as far as the conditions, well believe it or not – and I swear this is true – the bathroom actually smelled like pine. Mind you, it didn't smell *exclusively* like pine, but it was enough to convince me that I wouldn't get Chlamydia from sitting down and relieving myself. And while I'm sure that baseline levels of filth were restored soon after the show started, I didn't experience any weird rashes or burning sensations after that day.

So the show went on, I had fun, and we went home. When we pulled up to Handy Street that Sunday night, I was exhausted and filthy. After thanking the dudes, I walked briskly to the Rutgers bus stop and waited for my diesel chauffer to tote me back to college-land. I had a paper due the next day and hadn't started it.

At the time, I doubt that anyone had a clue as to how much of an impact Lifetime's music would ultimately have in the punk and hardcore universe; that a future generation of bands with significant mainstream success, like Fall Out Boy, Taking Back Sunday, and Saves The Day, would help elevate Lifetime to a position of vaunted respect within the genre. I sure didn't. I was just a kid who needed a ride.

With Spring on the way, Clothier Hall Student Government once again helped transform their dorm lounge into a place for punk rock to happen. This second time around, it was a much larger event. With bands alone, there were around thirty people; figuring in roadies and friends, the show felt extremely well-attended. And while I'm sure there were at least a few people who just accidentally happened upon the event, most of the people came because they were involved – materially, emotionally, or otherwise – in what was taking place.

And so the bands played their hearts out, and the kids were psyched, and it was good. There was Degradation, and instil, and Worthless. The Steadfasts had since broken up, but Zak had formed a new band with Fid called Suburban Manifesto, and they played. Prankster Pablo was involved with some band that played that night, called Measure for Measure. And a band called Velour 44 played, too. Overall, the night was awesome, and everyone seemed to have a good time. (Except instil, har, har.)

By the time the last band had finished playing, there was still time left on the room. So in an inspired "carpe-ing of the diem," various band members began running up and grabbing instruments. They swapped instruments and personnel repeatedly, improvising covers of classic punk rock songs that incited a qualified finger-pointing frenzy. There were pile-ons and epic sing-a-longs, and it was all totally spontaneous. We were caught up, in The Misfits, and Minor Threat, and Operation Ivy, and each other.

And it *felt* like something. At least to me.

I guess you can't write a book with New Brunswick in the title and not mention the grease trucks. Really, they're just six or seven lunch wagons parked in a lot on College Avenue – all with the same exact menu of artery-clogging delights, served into the wee hours of the morning. On the surface, pretty unimpressive. And yet, the trucks just can't be denied.

It starts when you get there. The dudes who work in the trucks – well, they're charged up and ready to sell you some falafel. They've got the Lebanese house music bumpin', and they're cat-calling the sexy college girls, and they're bro-ing down with all the college bros, and they might be drunk, and they're having a great fucking time. Hell, one of them might even sell you some weed out of the back of the truck. You never know.

Anyway, you walk into the center of the lot, and you're surrounded by trucks. And until you pick one, the dudes working in them all harass the shit out of you. It's the hard sell, taken to a new level. "Hey buddy, I make you cheese steak – hot like pussy!" Such "naughty" metaphors are (or at least used to be) standard grease truck material. If, for example, you ordered a turkey sub without mayonnaise, it might be repeated back to you as "turkey sub, no pussy juice." Very sexy.

But it's not just their more ephemeral charms that have distinguished the grease trucks as an institution in New Brunswick. It's the food.

Undoubtedly, the trucks' most famous offering is their line of "Fat" sandwiches. All of these not-so-little calorie bombs start off with a torpedo roll, but the actual substance of each individual sandwich varies (sort of) from one to the next. Each typically includes some combination of: beef patties, chicken fingers, French fries, mozzarella sticks, lettuce, cheese, onions, barbeque sauce, falafel, garden burgers, eggs, steak (and I don't mean a Porterhouse), shawarma, ketchup, mayo, and oregano. Originating with the Fat Cat (torpedo roll, two cheeseburgers, fries, tomatoes, onions, lettuce, ketchup, mayo, salt, pepper), these sandwiches have names like Fat Koko, Fat Darrell, Fat Balls and Fat Bitch, and they're all very, very bad for you. Still, it's arguable that the "New Brunswick experience" (ahem) isn't complete till you've tried one.

As one might expect, the combo of late hours and greasy food has made the trucks a universal downtime destination for New Brunswick's social elite; and/or, a beacon for drunken foolishness - without discrimination as to creed, color, or subculture.

Can you guess where this is going?

And so there we were, late one night at the grease trucks. It was me and Fid (blue hair and purple hair, respectively), along with some Skins - Tweety, Old Man Pedro, Doug and Rob. It was past 1:00 a.m., and foggy, and it had been a very low-key kind of night. Doug got his food first and walked back to his car to sit and eat. Somehow, as he haplessly opened the passenger-side door of his car, something happened. Either he'd lightly tapped the door of the neighboring car, or vice versa. It wasn't clear, but it didn't really matter because the guy from the other car was pissed, and not trying to hide it. He angrily accused Doug of hitting his car on purpose, which seemed to leave Doug baffled. Five seconds ago he planned to eat a sandwich, drive home, and probably go to sleep; now he was suddenly being accused of... *something*?

Now I don't know about anyone else who was there that night, but as words were exchanged, the picture quickly came clear to me. This had nothing to do with car doors or accidents. The dude from the other car was blatantly trying to provoke Doug. The other guy was black and Doug was a Skinhead.

Of course, the other dude had five friends with him, all dark-skinned too. And we... well, we were a group composed primarily of bald-headed, flight jacket-wearing Skinheads. It probably didn't look very cool.

The angry dark brown dudes started accusing the Skins of being white power boneheads; the Skins were immediately like, "Dudes, what are you talking about?" Pedro stepped to the front and announced his own Puerto Rican background as evidence that none of us were Nazis. And while it didn't take much explaining before some of the dark brown dudes slowly began to understand that they'd somehow made a mistake, a couple just didn't want to hear it. Maybe they were just drunk. Who knows? But from their words to their gestures, it was clear that they wanted one of our guys to throw a punch. A *first* punch.

Thankfully the Skins kept their composure, even as things seemed to escalate. After a few moments of arguing and yelling, the guy who had started the argument began to butt his chest up against Doug's, in that primal way that dudes square up. It seemed like the powder keg was about to be lit. Quickly, Pedro slipped his tall frame in between them, sandwiched with his face to Doug and his back to the dark brown guy. He threw his arms backwards over his shoulders, and pointed to a patch on the back of his flight jacket. It read, "SMASH RACISM."

But the guy *still* wouldn't back off. And if there was now a hint of hesitation in his voice, it didn't change anything; he didn't want to lose face. He'd taken the whole thing so far, and with such intensity, that backing out gracefully probably seemed impossible. Or maybe he was just drunk. Regardless, he kept yelling and pointing for a few seconds before his friends - confused but understanding that they'd somehow misread the situation - pulled him away. And that was that.

So luckily, a fight was avoided - and that was definitely a good thing. Not just for the obvious reason that, you know, violence is bad; but for the fact that, no matter who would have won the fight, the Skins would have lost out in the end. What would the headline have read? "Skinheads Clash With African Americans at Grease Trucks"?

Violence was like a poltergeist that year. And while there's all sorts of science that illustrates how kids seek out thrills and danger when they're in the throes of young adulthood, having Skinheads around can really provide a little extra oomph. Like hot peppers.

Still, I was an independent boy, and I didn't need help finding the threat of violence. In fact, I could find it just feet from my sock drawer - where, for example, an insane ex-convict pointed a gun at my head.

I'd been just coolin' in my dorm room when my next door neighbor Matt walked in holding his cordless phone. This wasn't unusual, since Matt walked into my room all the time. I was like, "Hey, dude what's up? I'll be right back – I'm going to the water fountain." He didn't say anything back to me and I figured that it was because he was listening to whoever was on the phone. I quickly walked past him and out into the hallway.

Then shit went south.

About three feet from me, I saw my next-door neighbor – a nice enough girl - being restrained forcibly by her beast of a boyfriend. And I guess he was pissed off about something, because he was holding a big silver gun. Having casually met the guy a couple of times in the past, he'd never really struck me as being very friendly, or very… centered? This was now confirmed.

Not wanting to upset the situation or die, my strategy was to appear as if I didn't care. After all, I didn't want to freak out in front of the guy, causing him to lose it and shoot someone. This meant that I couldn't just turn right around and go back into my room. That would have indicated that I was not "cool." So instead, I made eye contact with the maniac and continued stepping toward the water fountain. I leaned in, took a drink, turned around, and began the four-step journey back into the relative safety of my dorm room.

It was at step two, of course, when Angry Maniac, holding his struggling lady friend, aimed the gun at my head. Neither of us said a word, but the command was crystal clear: keep walking. I took a couple of automated, dreamlike steps toward and into my room, shut the door, and exhaled. Now I understood why my neighbor Matt had originally walked in without saying anything. After all, it wouldn't be very smooth to run in and scream, "Oh my god there's a dude with a gun out there and he's trying to kidnap Arlene!"

We were both pretty lucky. Locked inside my room, we called the cops and waited in a quiet panic. The girl was soon found in a nearby parking lot, having taken some damage. Prince Charming had gotten away, but a few weeks later he was arrested at a diner in a neighboring town.

Other than the near-shootings and non-racist almost-beatdowns, everything was pretty good. And as far as *Aneurysm* – well, things were steadily on the up-tick. By this point I'd pestered people for long enough that they were getting used to me and I was sending large stacks of zines to various distributors around the world. So in return for everyone's patience - and to keep them coming back for more - I spent most of the spring semester working on a new, bigger, better *Aneurysm*. It would abandon photocopies for newsprint and become the size of a proper magazine – all with more content ("interviews with Lifetime, instil, and more!") and a better layout than ever before. *Aneurysm* #9 was to be a watershed moment for my media obsession. I was on the war path.

As always, I was hitting as many shows as possible, which brought me to the Princeton Arts Council at the end of April to see instil and a bunch of other bands. It was a classic and typically diverse bill for the time, including the vampire-core of Philly's Ink and Dagger, the pop-punk of Princeton's own Sefler (who would soon mutate into Saves The Day), and the heavy, pissed hardcore of New Brunswick's own Endeavor.

I may have first heard of Endeavor through Zak, who grew up in the same area as guitarist Kevin Tunney. The band's harsh, screamy hardcore wasn't really Zak's speed, but he always spoke of them in a positive light; probably because Endeavor was a particular *type* of band – one that used music as a vehicle for certain types of very specific, often political messages. They were right up my alley. But while the band regularly played the New Brunswick area, I'd somehow never caught them. Nonetheless, I was in love with their recordings, so finally getting a chance to see Endeavor play live was something I'd been looking forward to.

Unfortunately, I arrived late and wound up missing almost all of their set. And while it surely wasn't the end of the world, I was still bummed. Regardless, I watched the other bands and had a good time. It was all pretty standard stuff – until Ink and Dagger played. With the lights out and lit candles placed around the stage, they slammed through their Swiz-inspired hardcore with maniacal aggression. Faces painted and strobe light pulsing, it was an approach that, in terms of aesthetic, was implicitly controversial within the confines of a scene that seemed to value deliberate realism. And the controversy became explicit once the band started tossing fake blood everywhere, staining the venue's ceiling, as well as the fancy dresses worn by some girls who'd apparently come to the show after attending a school dance.

But if witnessing Ink and Dagger's spectacle hadn't made up for missing Endeavor, I'd be able to make up for it two days later. They'd be opening for Avail and The Young Pioneers at the Wetlands in NYC. I was more than stoked - Avail was one of my very favorite bands, and finally getting to see Endeavor was the icing on the cake.

Unfortunately, it once again was not my night – or Endeavor's. Only a few songs into their set, an irreparable equipment problem ended everything with a dull thud. For all the internal hype I'd built up, I was once again bummed. But the show went on and I still could look forward to the other bands. And I figured that since the dudes in Endeavor were neighbors, I'd have plenty of other chances to catch their live show.

Another school year ended and more than anything I'd learned one thing – dorms were played out. The cold cement walls and random gun crimes had left a bad taste in my mouth. Ken and I had also worn thin on one another after two years and it was clear that moving on was definitely the right thing for both of us. So as Crawford and Tweety also sensed some flux in their living situations, the three of us planned to move in together. We found a house a couple of blocks behind the Rutgers Student Center, at 52 Wyckoff Street - a large place, with a back yard and plenty of room for parties. It certainly wasn't a palace, but it didn't suck.

In order to make the rent affordable, we needed a total of five housemates. One would be "Nick" Nicoletti, from 220 Hamilton. Nick wore big pants and was into wizards, crystals, getting fucked up and Life of Agony. Tenant number five was a kid named Andy. Tweety met Andy at the sleazy telemarketing company in downtown New Brunswick where they both worked. And while Andy might have seemed very straight-laced when stacked up against our little crew, he was nonetheless pretty fucking awesome - agreeing not only to share a house with us, but to share a *room* with Tweety; though he probably didn't know about the snoring like a wounded animal thing. Still, Andy was a very easy-going guy. Which was good; otherwise, he might not have survived the year that was to follow.

Four – 1995-1996: 52 Wyckoff

Tweety didn't have a whole lot of stuff to move – for the most part, only a bed, two dressers and a bunch of punk rock records – but he couldn't do it all by himself. And without any sort of real plan in place, things were looking sketchy. Tweety was, after all, supposed to be out of 220 Hamilton Street by midnight. He had nowhere to put his stuff other than the new place and the landlord would be showing up bright and early to turn the place over to its new tenants.

So on the evening of May 31st, 1995, Tweety gathered his regular crew of nine or ten Skinheads. They hung about, drinking and chatting as they waited for midnight to arrive. Midnight, after all, wasn't just the deadline for being out of 220 Hamilton – it was also the official start of the new lease at 52 Wyckoff. The witching hour and shit. So as midnight came and went, Tweety realized that he really had to go through with *something*. He and his friends loaded up a couple of cars with boxes and random stuff from the apartment. Then they made the quick trip across town to the new place.

American flag in hand, Tweety knocked on the door of 52 Wyckoff Street. At first, no one answered. But he kept knocking and the door was finally opened by the most perfectly scrawny kid of all time. Before the poor, stunned kid could get a single word out, Tweety stepped right into the apartment and in not so many words said, "Hey, it's June first - and we're moving in." Followed by ten (mostly) hulking Skinheads, he then stomped directly into the living room and stood on the couch next to another now-ex-tenant who had been sitting there half-asleep. Tweety pulled two pushpins from his pocket and tacked the large American flag to the wall.

Amazingly, there was actually someone less prepared than Tweety on moving day. It was the now-former residents of 52 Wyckoff Street. To be fair, their stuff *was* mostly packed up in boxes, which filled the kitchen. But tons of their crap was just lying around the house, not even close to packed. And as far as the kids themselves – well, moving out seemed like the last thing on any of their minds. They hadn't anticipated a late-night real estate dilemma – or ten raucous Skinheads barging into their house as they drifted off to Sleepy Land.

Without any clear alternatives, the kid who answered the door asked Tweety if it would be cool if he and his roommates could stay there until the morning, because they didn't have anywhere to go or a place for their stuff. It was a strangely familiar story. Tweety said that it was no problem, but that he and his ten friends had no intention of leaving the house to wait for its physical vacancy.

In fact, Tweety and his friends made themselves at home. They ate food and drank beer out of the refrigerator, started using the phone, and sat down on the couches in the living room to watch TV - all while the soon to be ex-tenants sleepily stood there, wondering what the hell was going on.

Fifteen minutes later, the ex-tenants started moving out. They were terrified. Skinheads, you know?

Which brings us to the Holocaust.

Back in the 1930s, both of my mom's parents fled their respective homes in Eastern Europe to escape Hitler's encroaching forces. Both landed in Palestine, which soon became Israel, where they eventually met and married, starting the family that would ultimately include my mother. They were the lucky ones who made it out. Almost all of their respective families – half of my bloodline – was murdered by Nazis.

So understandably, vigilance against anti-Semitism pervaded my childhood. The subject of the Holocaust was a conversational lightning rod; it could turn any casual chat with my mother into a dark and solemn remembrance, the program of which each time was sort of unpredictable. Sometimes she'd fume with bitterness and rage. Or she'd cry, crumbling under the weight of a sorrow that seemed impossible. Other times, Mom's voice would become small and her gaze distant – as she'd become visibly overwhelmed by her own feelings, thoughts, and memories. It wasn't like Mom talked about the holocaust all of the time – not at all. But when she did – well, it was *on.*

Mom's life, after all, was arguably the product of one of the most horrific human disasters in known history. The people who raised her – parents, community and nation – were positively chewed up and charred. By any calculation, it must have been a simply acrid childhood, stewing in the Holocaust's residual effects – pain, anger, fear and sadness. It defined her home, her friends, her school and her blood.

Not to mention the abject poverty. Mom's family got their first *out-house* when she was five years old. Up until then, the family had been shitting in a hole in the ground outside of their crude mud hut. Not fun.

My grandparents weren't poor when they lived in Europe, but the war had changed that. Their escape from the Nazis left them with absolutely nothing to their respective names, except a scant few surviving relatives, who couldn't really offer much help. Remember that scene in *Schindler's List,* where they're going through the boxes of teeth? It was like that.

So, yeah. Growing up, the Holocaust was big.

If, for example, a Holocaust-related program was going to be on television, you could bet that: 1) my mom would be watching, and 2) it would make her cry. I didn't like it. I was probably around 10 years old when I asked her why she watched things that made her so sad. The answer I got seemed smart enough. She said that she *had* to watch, so as to not let the memory and lessons of that tragedy die. But it wasn't her words that told me to back the fuck off – it was her intense, dark grief. At a core level, I somehow understood that I was asking about something I just couldn't understand. It was never easy, or comfortable.

Douchebags like Geraldo Rivera didn't help things. I mean, I myself had grown up thinking that Skinheads were Nazis, and were scary, and were evil. There was even a Nazi "Skinhead" in my high school who had confirmed this for me. For years, the mainstream media had been my only source of information on the topic. I never even considered that reality was, in fact, different than how it had been reported to me. No alternate possibilities existed to challenge what I thought I knew about Skinheads.But once I caught on, my understanding of the subject changed dramatically.

On visits home over those first couple of years, I'd occasionally attempt to talk to my parents about Skinheads, trying to debunk some of the bunk they believed relating to this particular subject. In theory, I should have wanted to do this because it was something cool for my parents to know about. But mostly, I was trying to make my own life easier. I knew that eventually, my mom and dad would be in the same room with some of my Skinhead friends – and I didn't want them to doubt for a moment that such an eventuality was safe and okay.

Conveniently, Old Man Pedro (ever the forward-thinker) had put together a small, photocopied informational booklet that served as a sort of *Skinheads for Dummies*. It explained the history of the Skinhead phenomenon and distinguished between Skinhead scenes, clarifying some of the messages perpetuated by irresponsible media outlets. Written in a friendly voice and featuring a cartoon Skinhead on the cover, the little booklet oozed with DIY charm; Pedro's little publication was as cute as it was informative.

So after two years of conversations and this booklet, push was now coming to shove. After all, I had to move all of my stuff into a house that would be teeming with Skins and there was no way my mother was not going to come check out her son's first apartment. I just had to hope that all my priming had done the job of cutting fear and misinformation off at the pass.

Move-in time arrived, and pulling up to the house at 52 Wyckoff on that beautiful June day became the moment of truth. The scene could not have been any more perfect. My parents and I pulled up in our Camry full of furniture and boxes to see a dozen or so tattooed Skinheads doing yard work and carrying stuff in and out of the house.

But shock and horror didn't take over as I thought they might. With only the slightest hint of hesitation, my folks met a number of my bald-headed friends – who, it turned out, were surprisingly warm people. Secretly, I was waiting for my mom's media conditioning to flip a switch in her head and make her think she was around a bunch of homicidal racists. But she didn't do any of that. Maybe it was the rainbow of skin colors present that made her question what she thought she knew. Had my preloaded disclaimers actually worked? Either way, the day went off without a hitch. My parents helped me move in, hugged me goodbye and left.

Smooth as butter.

As soon as my folks pulled away, of course, I learned that I'd only made it by the skin of my teeth. Earlier that morning, a particularly angry dude had flipped out and kicked the front door in. He'd destroyed the lock and damaged the door frame and we hadn't even been in the place for 24 hours. Luckily, this particularly angry dude had reached his breaking point and stomped off before my parents and I arrived. Had he stayed any longer, I might have had a whole lot of explaining to do. "Yeah, Mom and Dad, listen. Dramatic displays of violence aren't unusual among some of the people who hang out – especially when they've been drinking. But they're just sensitive, and misunderstood. And not Nazis."

In the first few months of our occupancy at 52, the house was constantly full of people. It might have gotten slightly out of hand at certain points, but playing host on this scale was new to me, so I just kind of went with the flow. Hell, even our landlord had greeted our arrival with a case of beer and some of his sucky home-grown pot. People came, and people went, and the house quickly took on a distinct electricity. We were even nice to the hippies who lived across the street.

But it wasn't all fun times in Unityville. For example, there was Doug.

Since our non-racist Skinheads-versus-Black Dudes encounter at the Grease Trucks some months back, Doug had come upon what some might call a time of transition. What this really meant was that he was living on our couch. He had a toiletry bag and everything. I'd known Doug for a while; he was a close friend of Tweety's, and a nice guy overall. And since the idea of having a couch to offer was still novel, I had no problem when Tweety asked/told the rest of us that we'd have a guest for a while.

But any illusions I had about opening my home in the spirit

of community were shattered the next day, when I entered the shower to find a used condom casually draped across my bar of Irish Spring. Enraged and completely skeeved out, I flew down the stairs and into the kitchen, demanding to know who had befouled my soap. Tweety laughed, noting that it had to have been Doug - the only person in the house who'd been with a girl the night before.

I carved a furious bee-line for Doug, who was in the living room. In disbelief, I demanded an answer: "Doug, did you leave a fucking used condom on my soap?"

"Oh, yeah," he said. "Sorry." He then blinked, looked away, and continued about his business. Fuck.

Especially at the start, the vast majority of people who came through 52 Wyckoff were Tweety's guests. And while most of these people were at least likeable – some even become close friends of mine down the line – the ones that sucked were really, really sucky. In one or two cases, they sucked because they said and did stupid things all the time. Or they sucked because they were ultra-violent and combative, not to mention strapped with muscles and/or knives. In Tweety's defense, lots of these people weren't really his "friends" as much as they were associates. And consistent with his character, Tweety almost always extended his hospitality, even to loosely-affiliated associates. Even if they kind of sucked.

The impromptu men's shelter in the living room wasn't the only annoyance at 52 Wyckoff Street. There was also the wondrous corner bedroom. Situated in the corner (duh) of the house, this room was only accessible by walking through either my room, or Crawford's. For the occupant of that room, it meant having to pick a roommate to irritate with each entrance and exit. Whether it was coming home drunk at 3 a.m. or going to the bathroom at 8 a.m., it was always annoying. Not to mention that my room and the corner room were separated by little more than a set of paper-thin folding doors. Really, it might as well have been one big room with those stupid hippie hanging beads dividing it in two.

It sucked for both me and Crawford, but the lack of privacy seemed to be par for the course. For the remainder of the year, anarchy would seem to permeate the house. Parties would erupt out of nowhere and I never knew what I'd be coming home to. At 7 p.m. on a Tuesday night, for example, I might have found thirty Skinheads watching soccer and punching holes in the living room walls.

There was pornography everywhere and bands would play in the kitchen. There was a black rubber dildo, and a number of people got beaten with it at various times. And once I saw a kid get suplexed (for real) right in my living room. It was a rare night when we didn't have at least one person sleeping on the couch; often it was three or four. Things were never boring. And considering that Fid, Jaime, Zak and some other kids had moved into a house at nearby 62 Guilden Street, it was like we had our own little punk rock neighborhood.

And that summer, New Brunswick was a great place to be a punk rocker.

At first glance, it didn't seem like much cause for celebration that one of New Brunswick's most vital punk rock venues would be shutting its doors. But in the case of 67 Handy Street, the end of one era meant the beginning of another. The residents of the house were indeed moving on, but ring leader Chris Ross planned to keep the music coming. Starting that August, the Melody Bar on French Street would pick up the slack, and Do It Youreself, all-ages hardcore and punk would continue to thrive in New Brunswick. So with something to look forward to, the last Handy Street show didn't quite feel like a sad goodbye; to me, it was more of a celebration.

And what a celebration they'd planned. Booking something like 14 bands, it was an insane lineup for any show, let alone one taking place in a basement: Sick Of It All, Lifetime, The Bouncing Souls, C.R., Fastbreak, Endeavor, Ensign and many more – and all for a meager three bucks.

Needless to say, the show was very well-attended; it seemed like there must have been a couple hundred people there. In terms of community and stuff, that sounds pretty good; in terms of crowd control, of course, it was a nightmare. In fact, there were people everywhere. This was in stark contrast to past Handy Street events, during which crowds were typically 1) smaller, and 2) very respectful of the rules and requests made by the people who actually lived at said address. These folks were, after all, opening their house to the community – with all the associated risks – so that people could come and enjoy punk and hardcore music in an open and intimate environment. And judging by how many shows took place there over the years, it's safe to say that things usually went just fine.

But this time, it just might have been too much. It didn't matter that Ross and the other people running things had repeatedly implored the crowd to stay in the basement or the back of the house. The kids just weren't listening and they did what they wanted to do. They milled about in front of the house and clustered in various spots on the block. It didn't take long for the neighbors to notice and then of course the cops, who in turn shut down the show before it was over. At which point the last Handy Street show became the first Handy Street show to be shut down by the man. It was a disappointment, especially because a number of bands, including the Bouncing Souls and Lifetime, didn't get to play. Yes, we still had the Melody Bar to look forward to; but it was still a vaguely depressing and anti-climactic way to send off such a beloved part of New Brunswick's punk and hardcore community.

But if the turnout for the last Handy Street show said anything, it was that the area's punk and hardcore scene was robust and pulsing. And nothing would demonstrate that more than what would happen at another show, one week later.

Now at the time, Earth Crisis was a bona fide force within the world of punk and hardcore. Informally, they occupied a top spot in the vegan/straight-edge segment of the national punk rock community, which was hitting a zenith in the second half of the 90s. But even as Earth Crisis' militant messages about substance use and animal rights polarized many of those involved with punk music, they were still just a band that played shows for the kids. And despite the occasional friction between members of the respective straight-edge and non-edge communities, people generally agreed to disagree.

Still, there were always exceptions. So when Earth Crisis was pelted with yogurt and beer cans while bringing the mosh at Middlesex County College that June, well, it wasn't necessarily a flashpoint - but people definitely took notice. Earth Crisis and their die-hard fans were plenty pissed (with good reason), while lots of other folks seemed to think that the incident was more funny than offensive. Some thought it was even funnier when they learned that one of the perpetrators was allegedly Ink and Dagger vocalist Sean McCabe. It wasn't that this new element necessarily defined the entire exchange, but it did seem to somehow make the incident more compelling - that the prank was facilitated, at least in part, by someone from another band; an accidental cultural ambassador, as opposed to just any old private citizen. At the time, I really believed in the ability of punk and hardcore to reclaim physical space - and in its ability to provide a venue for creative, purposeful expression and dialog. With this incident – its contrast of the mischievous and the sober (pardon the pun) as led by the front men of two very different yet similar hardcore bands – well, I believed that I was witnessing the promise of punk rock fulfilled.

Come on, man. I was 19 years old.

Despite all the awesomeness – the last Handy Street show, the yogurt conflict at Middlesex - the most important show of my summer was, without a doubt, the Skinhead Fish Fry.

Perhaps unsurprisingly, this event had nothing to do with fish. Instead, it was a bunch of bands playing at the M & M Hall, located in Old Bridge, a town located about 15 minutes outside of New Brunswick. The hall was an old, rustic lodge with a dirt parking lot, surrounded by trees. It reminded me of summer camp.

With both Worthless and Heidnik Stew on the bill, my attendance at the Fish Fry was guaranteed. There were many other people there, too – a low door price and the gaggle of young, outlandish bands likely having something to do with it. So I hung out, sold zines, and watched the bands. It was a pretty cool show, but fairly typical. That is, until *they* played; until I got bitch-slapped with some mighty hardcore punk. I'd never be the same again. Say it this way: *dee-JEN-err-iks*.

To be accurate, I had actually seen The Degenerics play once before, at The Stone Pony in Asbury Park. I really enjoyed their set - they were fast and angry, molding surf and hardcore and even ska into something pissed. There was something about The Degenerics that emanated a certain old-school essence - they reminded me of the Bad Brains and Minor Threat, and that got my attention.

But this time at the M & M Hall – well, it was simply furious, and they sounded amazing. Their speed, their precision, their power – there was a certain abandon in The Degenerics' performance that made the other bands that day seem like cardboard clowns by comparison. I was a believer.

After their set I made sure to talk to the dudes in the band. I gave them some zines, they gave me a demo, and we hung out. I talked to the guitar player, Frank, the most. He was warm and outgoing and seemed really... I dunno, *nice*. And it turned out that we had even played a show together – which was weird, because I'd only played like four shows in my entire life. Nonetheless, it was true – Frank had been the singer of the Missing Children, who'd played with the Lost Boys a year prior. I don't know if that qualifies as a coincidence, but we thought it was cool.

Craig was The Degenerics' vocalist, and I'd actually met him before, too, at WRSU. Having been something of a manager for the Missing Children, Craig had once come to the station with Frank to help promote the band on Tweety's show. And while at the time, I didn't sense anything extraordinary about the kid, that had now changed dramatically. When it came to performance, Craig was a human explosion.

It wasn't even his actual vocals that commanded attention when Craig performed. (Not that vocal ability necessarily had anything to do with being the singer of a punk rock band, anyway.) No, Craig was amazing because he demonstrated such extreme emotion, using his entire physical body as an instrument of expression and – incidentally – entertainment. And while he might have just been a kid screaming his head off, in many ways art doesn't get more pure than what Craig did.

A skinny kid named Pat played bass. Pat was a skater with some cool tattoos and a quick wit, and was super psyched about The Degenerics. He loved clever turns of the phrase, kitchy slang and *The Simpsons*. Despite Pat's constant sarcasm, there was still something earthy about him. As I'd learn, he was (at least in some respects) incredibly industrious. Patrick was, after all, the manufacturing arm of The Degenerics, largely responsible for all things silk-screened (although he did get some occasional help).

And the drummer – well, his name was really Brian, but nobody called him that. He was P-Nut, spelled exactly that way, and yes – the name had everything to do with his small physical stature. P-Nut had an outstanding personality; he was an unavoidable, fiery spirit, and an atypically talented drummer.

It was a great night. The show was packed and kids were running around being silly, dancing and singing along. You can debate the value of real versus imagined experiences all you want, but that afternoon I felt a spirit in the air. I was with my friends, making new ones, and shit was working the way it was supposed to. We were reclaiming that space. We were celebrating community, and expression, and rock and roll. For a raving mad idealist, it made this old lodge into a Utopia.

The last band of the evening finished playing and loaded their gear out of the M & M Hall. Out in the parking lot, it didn't seem like anyone wanted to go home; all the kids from the show just chatted and milled around instead of getting in their cars and leaving. It was a question mark. So as dusk rolled the day into night, Tweety offered the answer. Spontaneously and loudly, he announced that the after-party would be at our house. All those within earshot, of course, were invited.

Standing with The Degenerics, I enthusiastically reiterated the invitation. They accepted on the spot, and it was clear – we were all genuinely stoked to be hanging out with one another. It was a down home moment.

That evening, almost everyone from the show did, in fact, arrive at my house. It was the first real party at 52 Wyckoff Street, and the first of many nights in which neighbors would peer outside nervously from behind tightly drawn curtains, probably thinking things like, "Why did that one Nazi throw that other Nazi into my windshield?", or "Is that guy lying in the yard dead or just passed out?" For what it's worth, things often sounded much worse than they really were.

But that *first* night, as I consider it, was more than just a party; it was a gathering. There were drunk punk rockers and Skinheads everywhere – sober ones, too. There were angry, destructive types, and easy-going kids just looking to have a good time. There was activism, and there was apathy. Future lawyers and future porn stars. And we were all there together.

As for the party itself – well, it was expectedly insane. Small cliques who came from the show began to convene and mesh with others. Boys met girls. People drank and smoked and ate and sang along with whatever was on the stereo. Friends were made. For many of the people who were there, that night is remembered as a flashpoint of sorts; the first few lines of some kind of chapter. Shit, we weaved a motherfuckin' tapestry of life. And that night, 52 Wyckoff became something vaguely more than just a punk rock flophouse.

And The Degenerics – well, they hung out into the wee hours of the morning, and we had a blast. Between shared tastes, sarcasm, and our love for punk rock, we just got along really well.

A big piece of our common ground was in how we related as individuals to the music that occupied so much of our respective time. One must remember that the so-called "definition" of Punk Rock has been hotly debated for a long, long time; thousands of years if I'm not mistaken. And thanks to the subjectivity of human expression, lots of interpretations emerge; variations on a theme, if you will. The result is that punk rock can look and sound like a lot of different things. Maybe I was so mentally attracted to The Degenerics because their interpretation of punk was one I related to on a level I'd not found in any of my other friends. So many of the punk rockers I already knew were negative people, or didn't care about anything, or just didn't see things in any way that was compatible with mine – but not The Degenerics. They were refreshingly positive; and I, too, was on that tip.

Perhaps nothing better demonstrated why I loved The Degenerics better or more explicitly than their adoption of the slogan "P.M.A."

"P.M.A." – or, "Positive Mental Attitude" - first found its way into punk and hardcore through the Bad Brains, who'd incorporated the concept into their songs and record layouts after finding God in 1979. Originally, the abbreviation and its implicit concept were coined by American author Napoleon Hill; his most well-known book - *Think and Grow Rich* – is arguably the first modern self-help book; it's also one of the best-selling texts of all time.

Understandably, the thrust of P.M.A. - to help oneself find success, to learn from failure, to fear no obstacle, and all kinds of other sensible but obvious sort of shit – was a solid match for angry kids who wanted to change the world. And since, at the time, The Degenerics rocked the aforementioned Bad Brains influence (even covering both "Attitude" and "Supertouch/Shitfit"), co-opting "P.M.A." just sort of completed the package. Anyway, there are worse things to be into. And it was convenient to have a handy little slogan that could help me confirm and qualify the affirming connection I'd made with my new homies.

From that first night - the Skinhead Fish Fry after-party - it felt like The Degenerics and I had been down for years. It was, in fact, the beginning of a strong and storied brotherhood. I wound up going to almost every show they played over the next few years. I sold their merchandise, helped carry their equipment at shows and put them into the pages of *Aneurysm*. And of course, I sang along.

After all, there was a lot I could learn from these dudes. They had been down with punk rock a lot longer than me, and they were into a number of bands I'd never really explored. Then there was The Degenerics' mastery of the D.I.Y. arts - the stickers, patches, and demo tapes in bulk, made by hand with simple but effective tools. In time, the band's industrial arm in and of itself would become powerful. Not only did their signature asterisk logo become a ubiquitous sight in the NJ punk scene, but the intensity of the band's manufacturing campaign likely inspired other folks in our little community to turn up the juice on their own creative projects.

My punk rock dream was perpetually coming true right before my eyes. Zines, houses, bands, shows and more friends than I'd ever had in my entire life. And it all just seemed to be getting better and better.

Although I'd spent most of the summer in New Brunswick, Chad and I still managed to hang out regularly. So as autumn drew closer, I decided to spend a few last days in Marlton, hoping to get in some quality chill time before school started back up; not to mention the added mission of acquiring some supplies from my parents.

Marlton was fun enough and hanging out with Chad was awesome. But I spent most of my brief visit wondering what I was missing back in New Brunswick. And by the Saturday of my scheduled return to the Hub, I was raring to go. I hurriedly packed my parents' car with the usual provisions – soda pop, clean clothes, junk food, toilet paper – and then practically pushed my mom and dad out the door so we could leave. I didn't think at all that such behavior might have been considered rude or ungrateful; I was in the throes of compulsion, driven to return to a place where I felt (or imagined that I felt) a kind of sacred and growing energy.

Remember that old Tootsie Roll commercial where the kids sing about how everywhere they look, they sees Tootsie Rolls? *"Whatever it is I think I see/Becomes a Tootsie Roll to me."* A kid looks at a train, but sees a Tootsie Roll. Another kid looks at a whale, she sees a Tootsie Roll. Et cetera. That was me. Except that, instead of Tootsie Rolls, I saw the potential for revolutionary social upheaval. These were my punk rock rose colored glasses, they were fucking shatterproof, and everything was awesome if it was punk rock. My friends and I were the bringers of truth, expression and promise. Rushing my folks out the door might have seemed rude, but I had to get back to the think tank. To the enclave.

So we rolled into New Brunswick about an hour later and I was stoked to be back. Summer still had some breath in her lungs and I was even looking forward to the imminent start of the fall semester. As my parents and I rounded the corner onto Wyckoff Street, my head and heart were full of stuff.

Then something caught my eye. Alright, "caught my eye" is an understatement. You know when a cartoon character sees something wacky and his eyes pop out of his head and go "Aooooooo-gah!"? It was like that.

What I'd forgotten was that this particular Saturday was Tweety's birthday, and that he'd planned a barbeque to mark the occasion. In the moments before my parents and I turned the corner, a dispute between two guests over a parking spot had escalated into a full-fledged street fight. In the broadest of August daylights, the entire party at 52 Wyckoff had poured into the street. The street fight became a riot - and I was rolling up to it with my parents. I suddenly noticed a scratch on my rosy glasses.

It could have been worse - much. Thanks to some lucky timing, we'd caught the tail end of the brief brawl. As my parents and I rolled slowly down the street, the crowd quickly dispersed so that by the time we were in front of the house it was completely gone. And my folks? Well, somehow they just... didn't notice! It was amazing, really. Maybe it hadn't registered in their minds, or maybe they just weren't looking in the right direction. Either way, I considered it something of a miracle. I mean, there were, like, 25 people involved, fighting in the street right in front of us – and my parents just kind of missed it. Insane.

One dude who didn't dodge his bullet that day was The Wolff. He caught a bottle to the head courtesy of Tweety, and he didn't deserve it.

I'd only met The Wolff once before the riot, but he seemed like a cool enough dude. He and Pat from The Degenerics had once played together in a spastic hardcore band called K.G.B. (which supposedly stood for "Kids with Good Barbers"). The Wolff was a few years older than the rest of us and something of a reformed troublemaker. To me, he seemed like the kind of guy who would buy beer for his underage friends, and then make sure that no one choked on their own vomit. To be sure, The Wolff came off as one of the good ones.

So when The Degenerics needed help, The Wolff was there.

Eager to grow the band, they planned their first real out-of-town show. Booked at the Rathskeller in Boston, The Degenerics would be playing with Philadelphia's Violent Society, as well as local acts The Unseen and The Ducky Boys. It was an exciting proposition, with just one problem. The Degenerics didn't have a van and none of the members were old enough to rent one.

But The Wolff was. So even though he wasn't going on the trip, he stepped up to use his oldness for the forces of good. Of course, there's probably something illegal about renting a vehicle and then letting kids with fireworks drive it to Boston, unsupervised. But that didn't bother any of us.

It *was* troubling, however, on the morning of our planned departure when The Wolff pulled up to Pat's house in a Honda Accord, as opposed to the minivan we were expecting. It turned out that the rental place had somehow run out of vans and this sport sedan was the best they could do. So with no better alternative, the five of us piled into the Accord, stacking all kinds of very heavy equipment onto our laps. Guitars, amp heads, drums – you name it, it was on our laps. And yes, it sucked as much as one might imagine.

Still, it all felt like a momentous adventure. I was toughing it out on a do-or-die mission to Boston, a city I'd never visited, and one of the oldest strongholds of American hardcore music. Not only was I with friends, or with a band – I was with my friends' band, and they came to destroy. It gave me a sense of ownership, participation and adventure I'd never experienced.

I just wish we'd planned better.

Earlier, the decision had been made to arrive in Boston the night before the show; a sensible measure, taken as a precaution against arriving late and blowing the opportunity all together. But in a truly baffling display of youthful short-sightedness, we'd arrived in town that Friday evening with no accommodations. And though we pulled into Boston yelling absurdities at pedestrians and whizzing through traffic, our posture soon became a bit more humble. We were suddenly five dudes from Jersey, in the middle of Boston with nowhere to go.

Hoping to find a hostel or a YMCA to sleep at that evening, we searched the city up and down, exhausting all possibilities and turning up empty. Even the local crusty kids we met on the street couldn't help us get situated. Having banked on a minivan, our last resort had originally been to sleep in the vehicle that night. But because of the equipment and the fact that the vehicle was now a fucking Honda Accord, that option could no longer accommodate all five of us. Don't let anyone tell you otherwise – it's impossible to relax with a floor tom on your lap.

With the equipment shuffled around, the car could sleep three at a time, sort of. So we broke the night into shifts. Frank, Pat and Craig slept first, while P-Nut and I sat on the curb for hours, smoking cigarettes and watching rats scurry by in the unusually bright Boston night. At around 3:30 a.m., our shift came up and we woke up our sleeping friends to claim some sedan time. But within a few hours, the heat and noise of the city had made sleep impossible. Tired and smelly, it was now 9:30 a.m., and the five of us were now resigned to waiting until the show started that afternoon. We headed down to Kenmore Square, where we "showered" in a McDonald's bathroom and bummed cigarettes off of strangers to pass the time. It wasn't a very dignified morning, and we were exhausted, but it was a lot of fun.

Anyway, The Degenerics played and so did the other bands. And beyond the regular fun of a good, wholesome punk rock show, I was otherwise invigorated. I was at a dirty club in a strange city, watching my friends tear it up. I was psyched to be selling their merch (and my zines) to kids we'd never met before. And I was psyched to be a part of a unit, in any capacity. Perhaps most of all, it was an honor to help provide something to kids the way I felt it had been provided to me. Here we were – five dudes from New Jersey, and a band no one knew, in a strange city. It was an adventure.

Over the course of the evening, The Degenerics and Violent Society hung out a lot. So when Mike and Pat from Violent Society learned that we needed a place to sleep that night, they hooked us up. They took us to an apartment in nearby Allston. The guy who lived there was in a band called the Showcase Showdown, and he offered us a little bit of hospitality. My personal accommodations consisted of a filthy mattress on a kitchen floor and a smelly dude next to me. It was the best situation I'd had all weekend. The next morning, we went home tired, dirty, and eager to do it all again and again.

Despite all of its varied awesomeness, the summer of 1996 was not impenetrable. While many students dread the return of school each fall, that year I was really looking forward to it. Amazingly, my first two years of classes at Rutgers were really enjoyable. Sure, there were some annoying or uninteresting graduation requirements. But as opposed to high school, where classes were the same for everyone, at college I was able to study what I wanted to study – which worked out for me. I was suddenly compelled to declare a double major, in both Political Science and Journalism/Mass Media.

Given my long-standing media obsession, the Journalism degree seemed like a no-brainer. Unfortunately, most of the people I met at the Rutgers journalism school also seemed like no-brainers. I did the work, of course, but to say that I was "into it" might be a little generous. The truth was that countless things about the field, my colleagues and most of the professors turned me way, way off.

On the other hand, I'd become deeply involved – intellectually, psychologically and emotionally – with Political Science. It made sense. Almost all of my favorite music echoed ideas once offered by the great thinkers I'd been exploring. To me, this lent a particular credibility to punk and hardcore. I believed that, whether they knew it or not, the kids with their bands and zines and stuff were – often perhaps accidentally - reflecting the same real-world struggles discussed by the world's best-known political philosophers. From Hobbes and Locke to Machiavelli to Rousseau to John Stuart Mill – from Bad Religion and Los Crudos to Embrace and Jawbreaker and Propagandhi – the connections were everywhere.

And - please forgive the joke - my buck stopped with Karl Marx. When it came to how I saw life, community and art – well I'd never encountered ideas as compelling as *The Manuscripts of 1848*; *Capital*, *Theses on Freurbach*, and of course, the (short and easy-to-read) boogeyman of written word, *The Communist Manifesto*. These works and others had caused dramatic, fundamental changes in how I perceived the world and my place in it. And while the compromises and material realities of my particular adult life would eventually cause me to pull back a bit, back then it was clear. I was a "Marxist."

So it was a convergence of influences, from 19th century social philosophy texts to Minor Threat, which helped me come to a self-styled, personal revelation of sorts: the world urgently needed a unified understanding of the relationship between the personal and the political. I was suddenly convinced that people would care more about changing the world if they understood exactly how particular injustices affected their own individual lives.

Let's qualify all of this glitter. I don't know how it's gone for other folks, but my life at 20 year old felt like a continuous explosion. Yeah, it's an age around which many American kids start to carve out an "adult" existence, so changing dramatically at this time in one's life certainly isn't unheard of. But between punk rock and all of those social philosophy books, it felt like I was being rebuilt from the ground up. While Marx, Locke and all of the others certainly weren't the definitive word on how "everything" works, reading their ideas was teaching me to think in new, bigger and arguably better ways; and teaching me to always question what I think I know. Coupled with the onset of American adulthood, it signaled a dramatic shift in how I understood the things that upset me. It was the difference between hating a cop because of domination, social hierarchy, et cetera, or hating the *idea* of a cop with the understanding that the person in that uniform is a frightened, hungry little human being, just like you and me. For sure, I was changing.

I guess all of that growing up made me feel pretty fancy. I suspect that a few other people were feeling fancy back in those days, too. Our little community was, after all, a group effort, and the kids around me were in midst of growing up too. Maybe it was just what I wanted to see, but I think that a number of people were genuinely energized by being who they were, where they were. So maybe it was inevitable that we would try to somehow organize all of this scattered creativity. Or maybe it was just because I knew that a club might need a newsletter. Either way, a few people (myself included) agreed to form a punk rock collective in order to, you know, collect us. We envisioned some sort of association that would somehow encourage D.I.Y. punk rock-type people to build upon one another's efforts, and to grow our little hardcore punk community. For a name, Crawford came up with The Boots and Roots Collective of New Jersey; beyond being united, our goals were not clear.

There were a couple of meetings, both of which were surprisingly well-attended; we probably had 30 people show up the first time. If memory serves, the majority of that first meeting was spent trying to figure out how to conduct meetings. Would we have some sort of parliamentary procedure? Maybe a talking wand. Would we have rules? *Could* we have rules? What would

Suburban Manifesto - Clothier Hall, 1996 (Photo: Jen Ball)

The Degenerics - American University, Washington D.C., 1997

The Degenerics - Milltown, NJ, 2000

Stormshadow - A church in Trenton, NJ, circa 1997

Strength691 (last show) - Middlesex County College, 1996

*The Degenerics - a basement somewhere in America, 1997
(photo: unknown)*

The Degenerics - Pizza Hut, New Brunswick, 1997

Pedro Angel Serrano - Mason Gross School of The Arts, 1999

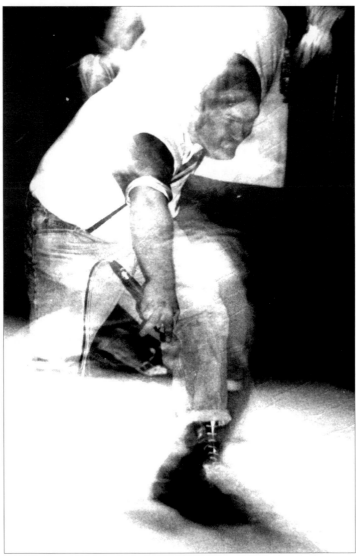

Heidnik Stew - Livingston College Student Center, 1996

The Degenerics - The Palace, Bound Brook, NJ 1998

Rock,Star - The Melody Bar, 2000 (photo: Troy Esposito)

Worthless - Bates Lodge, Red Bank, N.J. 1997 (Photo: Jen Ball)

*try.fail.try - The Westwood garage, Westwood, NJ, 1997
(photo: S. Filippi)*

Endeavor (last show) - The Melody Bar, 1998

Endeavor (last show) - The Melody Bar, 1998

The Purpose - Technical Ecstasy Sound Complex, 1998

try.fail.try - Middlesex County College, 1997

You and I - A church in Trenton, N.J, 1997

Lifetime - last Philadelphia show, the Trocadero, 1997

Bouncing Souls - The Palace, Bound Brook, 1999

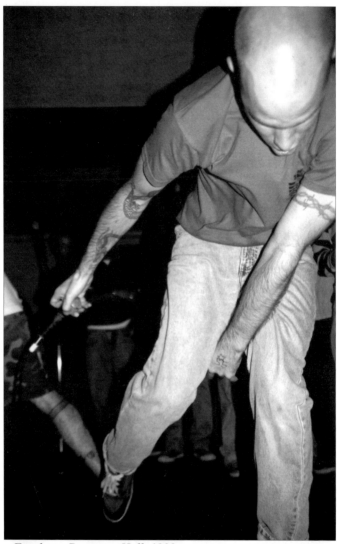

Fanshen - Demarest Hall, 1999

Flyers from various shows around New Brunswick in the 1990s

/Aneurysm/ fanzine – final issue, 1997

they be? What were we doing there in the first place? What was the point of all of this?

In all fairness, a number of great shows *were* put on under the Boots and Roots banner and at least a couple of them were benefits that raised money for one worthy cause or another. And admittedly, trying to organize a room full of people who fancied themselves as individuals and/or rebels was tricky business, despite any ideals of scene unity or other such stuff. And it was quite possible that we simply didn't need a formal body to be "together," so there was that. Whatever the reasons, it wasn't long before the formal body known as The Boots and Roots Collective of New Jersey stopped existing altogether. And despite (or maybe because of) my drunken idealism, I walked away from the experience not feeling too shattered.

Did I really have hope that a bunch of kids from New Jersey could thrust economic justice and peaceful autonomy on the world? Did I believe that my crew was some sort of spontaneous think-tank/freedom march? An anarchist commune, disguised as a bunch of college kids and their friends? Maybe I envisioned all of this and more – but I like to think that, deep down, I knew better.

The paradox, of course, is that it was still very important to me that kids and bands pulled the most they could from punk rock and hardcore; that they built an intellectual space and used it to the threshold of its potential. It's just that by this point I was learning that the pitfalls were everywhere; for example, that it didn't take much to be in a band and play shows. On the other hand, making it count – making it real and urgent and passionate – well, that was a respectable pursuit. It was a golden standard, and my ideal – that an exchange of critical ideas could be wrapped up in music, fun and self-expression.

Full of hope and psyched for the future, I rededicated myself to, like, life and shit. Foremost, I resigned to be as focused as possible on my work – academic, artistic and otherwise. Yes, this kind of enthusiasm in some ways seems to contradict some of punk's most primal tendencies – boredom, disengagement, self-destruction. Really though, those interpretations of punk had only appealed to me in concept. In practice, I was an outspoken, involved individual. I once read a quote that said: "If punk is 'I won't' then hardcore is 'I will.'" While I've never agreed with the wholesale characterization of punk as lazy or apathetic, the sentiment still kind of made sense. Although I didn't know exactly who I wanted to be, I knew what I didn't want to be.

Despite having spent years with my cynicism and anger way out in front, empathy now washed over me. It had been there all along, of course – I just didn't get it. But now, regardless of any social transgressions I'd committed in the past, I felt like I got it and I was almost ashamed to have existed before having gotten it. The problems of those around me (and those far away) became more troubling than ever and in my mind, I strove to become what I might have called "an agent of social change." Music was my fuel; I continued and intensified my search for those bands with the most overt socio-political lyrics. At the time, it seemed like there were plenty of them to be found.

Now that's not to say that the scene was dominated by politics, because it wasn't. But I perceived a certain psychological or emotional honesty about many of the bands at the time. Even bands that I couldn't relate to – Krishna bands, for example – appeared to be making an earnest attempt to trade in ideas as much as in music. From literature at merch tables to speeches between songs, lots of bands were using their visibility to bring up social and political issues. Some of the bands themselves even seemed almost secondary to the messages they delivered, with the music becoming more of a tool than anything else. This was music that existed in an urgent context – and at a time when most of the mainstream was Everclear and the *Macarena*, it was comforting to know that not everything sucked.

Fall hit its stride and things seemed to calm down (at least slightly) at 52 Wyckoff Street. The endless stream of dudes living on our couches, however, continued unabated. After Doug's condom-riffic tenure, a number of other individuals graced us with their slumber. There was Robert, Rob and Rory (RIP). Old Man Pedro lived with us for a while, and Pat from The Degenerics stayed at 52 a lot, too. It wasn't the most serene environment, but that was okay because the order of the day was community.

There was a big Halloween show at the Edison Elks Lodge that year, in nearby (and scenic) Edison, New Jersey. Once again, it was a bill that included both Ink and Dagger and Endeavor, with HeartBreak, All Else Failed, Puritan and Face of the Assassin rounding out the bill. But beyond it being a big local show with the then-uber-controversial Ink and Dagger, I had arranged to interview Endeavor for *Aneurysm*.

Since Endeavor was scheduled to play later in the show, I scheduled the interview for early in the evening. Meeting in their van, I sat down with the band and a kid named Carl - he was their homeboy and had put out Endeavor's first seven inch on his then-tiny record label, Ferret Music. We did the interview, which was intensive and thorough. In step with what was then my desire to link punk rock with my academic interests, I asked a lot of questions about the band's politics. After all, Endeavor were a band after my own heart – heavy, pissed, and loaded with hard political content. And overall the interview went very well. Vocalist Mike O. and guitarist Kevin Tunney had the most to say, but everyone in the band seemed to be smart, funny, friendly, funny and funny.

Like, for example, when Ink and Dagger played later that night. To be fair, those kids had to know what they were walking into. It had only been a few months since vocalist Sean McCabe had allegedly tossed a Yoplait at Earth Crisis as they rocked Middlesex County College; and only a few months before that, they'd brought the aforementioned noise and blood-stained ceiling at the Princeton Arts Council.

So it shouldn't have been a surprise that their set came with some complications. As mentioned previously, Ink and Dagger was huge on the stage show – candles, strobe lights, darkness. And while elements like these did serve to polarize some folks, such multi-sensory effects were nonetheless a defining component of the band's undeniable presence and mystique. So they were probably pissed off when someone turned on the lunch room-like fluorescent lights in the middle of their set. As the song they were playing ended, McCabe expressed his displeasure with the lights being turned on and the darkness was reinstated. Ink & Dagger launched into their next song, but moments into it the darkness and ambience were once again dissolved by the switching on of the house lights. Determined to figure out who was pulling this incredible prank, my eyes darted to the back of the room - where I saw Endeavor guitarist Kevin Tunney standing a few scant feet from the light switch. He looked at me and smiled subtly.

The song ended, and the joke had run its course. Visibly annoyed, McCabe spoke with great consternation: "Let's play a little game. Turn on the lights, turn off the lights." While I suppose he was implying that the prank was somehow droll or mundane, I thought it was pretty fucking funny – *and*, a clever and creative use of the space provided within the more esoteric definitions of punk rock. So there.

K.G.B. had never played a proper last show, and The Wolff wanted to change that. Determined to make it happen, but without a venue at his immediate disposal, he managed to track down a Masonic temple with an affordable rental hall in the nearby town of Metuchen. A few shows had taken place there in the past, though the place would hardly have been considered a consistent venue. So once The Wolff's show went off without any problems, it wasn't long before more were being booked – not just by The Wolff, but by Crawford, Craig, myself and others. With access to a cheap, reliable space, the steam gathered. The Masonic Temple in Metuchen began to emerge as a real asset to D.I.Y. hardcore and punk in the Middlesex County area.

The space wasn't huge – 200 people would have packed it tightly. And the sound was never awesome. But people consistently came out and it wasn't just our friends. For many of the local kids, we were providing a first encounter with live punk and hardcore music, and ideas. With a lot of hard work, the temple started to become a place where industrious creativity could thrive. While the first bands to play were our own, it wasn't long before touring bands were coming through on a regular basis. From San Diego and Richmond, Philly and Staten Island, and everywhere in between - they came. And we went with it.

Yet something was missing. Sure, I enjoyed booking shows and making flyers. I enjoyed being a roadie and selling merchandise. *Aneurysm* was doing well and I'd even begun planning to put out a record (Worthless' first seven inch, *The Revenge of Doctor Stanley*, featuring Zak as the band's new guitarist). But there came a point when something changed. All around me people were getting to write songs, go on tour and make records - and I wanted that too. True, I had experienced playing music with friends by that point in my life, but none of those attempts had yielded anything meaningful, or memorable; at least, not in a good way.

And I was sick of writing *about* music; I wanted to *play*. I wanted to stop theorizing like so many armchair rock stars; to stop writing the record reviews I'd otherwise call bullshit, to stop searching for adjectives and go try it all for myself, but for *real* this time. Not to mention that formal writing, which had long been my focus, was now losing some of its appeal; probably because, as noted earlier, so many of my experiences at *Targum* and the Rutgers journalism department had left awful tastes in my mouth. And if I had learned to distrust the media and its managers in such an encompassing sense, then entertainment media was my Great Satan.

Right. I'd spent enough time feeling like a spectator, so I joined a band.

Somehow – the exact details are fuzzy - I was put in touch with a bunch of slightly older dudes who were really into the driving, melodic material associated with bands like Samiam and Farside. While my tastes at the time leaned toward more abrasive material, I was still down with such melodic post-core, so I figured it would be fun. The guys themselves were complete strangers and that was a little weird; not to mention that they had already been through four singers.

But Luke, John, Tim and Mike turned out to be cool dudes. We knew a few people in common, and two of them were South Jersey transplants like me. These were comforting tidbits in the first moments of what was otherwise an awkward proposition – meeting four strangers and attempting to play music with them.

But we did it. Down in the basement of their house on High Street, I listened to their music and wrote some vocals. And it felt cool when the guys offered me the position of lead vocalist, even though (or maybe because) we were strangers.

We got to know each other throughout the process of putting the songs together. In some cases, that might be called the "songwriting process," but here I don't think it's an accurate description. After all, these dudes had been playing together for a while and subsequently had *plenty* of material, were well-practiced and ready to go. So the songwriting process seemed mostly to be a matter of how fast I could get the lyrics and vocal melodies together.

Within a couple of months we played our first show under the name Redshift at the original Cheap Thrills record store on George Street. Cheap Thrills was a decent record store and something of an institution in New Brunswick, but not well known for having live shows. Regardless, I'd been there countless times over the past few years and so at least I'd be making my New Brunswick vocal debut in familiar territory. We played okay, if not for a small bit of the usual slop you might expect at any band's first show. I sang it like I meant it and no one threw a tomato or spit on me; by all accounts, a qualified passing grade.

The band that played after us was called Nora and it was their first show, too. Nora was full of familiar faces. Handy Street dude and now Melody Bar hardcore show maestro Chris Ross was the drummer. Spliedt, who I first met the previous year in Lifetime's van, was the bass player. Endeavor vocalist Mike O. was playing guitar. And Carl, who I originally met when interviewing Endeavor that past Halloween, was the singer. Their other guitar player, Murph, was the only member I didn't know.

As far as first shows, it could have been much worse for Redshift. So it was with at least some degree of confidence that we went forward, booking more shows and starting to get focused.

But some things just can't be forced, and I saw repeated signs that Redshift just wasn't the band for me. Like at the Melody Bar on New Years' Eve, going into 1997, when that drunk guy miraculously sang along to every song we played – even though we'd never recorded and it was only our second show. Or like a few days later, when we played to a mostly empty, entirely disinterested room at the Stone Pony in Asbury Park. It was a nice gesture from Craig, who had hooked us up with the show. But that didn't make anyone care about Redshift – not even me.

For the most part Redshift was doomed by the old, reliable artistic differences. The band's material was good, but it didn't speak to me. At the time, I was into loud, fast, and heavy – the more the better – and this band clearly wasn't going that direction. I really did want to be in a band – just not this particular one. And it showed. Soon enough, I was cutting practices and even shows. Once, I even bailed on a show last minute, just so I could go to scenic (read: corpse-like) York, PA with The Degenerics. I quit Redshift the next day; some of the guys got pissed, and that was that. Eventually Redshift would find a new singer, change its name to Ex-Number Five, and do just fine.

I was bummed, but I also knew that joining any old band that would take me wasn't the best solution. It had to be the *right* band, and the music had to make me *feel* something. In that sense, I knew that I couldn't force or rush anything. Still, carrying equipment and selling t-shirts made me antsy. I knew that I had to find a band. *My* band.

In the meantime, though, I had the Degenerics – and in many ways, I was living vicariously through them. Okay - maybe that's not the best description. After all, "living vicariously" implies that I was simply imagining what it felt like to actually *be* a Degeneric. But as individuals, Craig, Pat, Frank and P-Nut had become four of my very closest friends. And maybe because they'd invited me to spend so much band-related time with them; not like I showed up to practice twice a week or anything, but they could count on me - to sell t-shirts, or hold the money, or carry some gear. I was always down. There was, of course, the one glaring exception to this, which was when The Degenerics actually played their music. But I never felt excluded, or even close to it. I was, after all, The Degenerics' biggest fan (at least as far as I knew); and getting to see them perform was always the shit.

So when Craig informed me that the band wanted me to come on their first real tour - well, I was stoked. We'd be heading south for spring break, punk rock style. It was pure awesome, and as the time of the tour drew closer, anticipation grew amongst The Degenerics and associated company.

By the time March of '97 rolled around, Craig and Pat had ironed out a 10-day itinerary, taking us through Virginia and the Carolinas, all the way to Florida and home again. A van was reserved and paid for. The band stocked up on t-shirts, stickers, and patches. Everything was set and ready to go.

And then, once again, on the morning of our planned departure – drum roll, please – Frank simply bailed out. His reason had something to do with money. He was, after all, a 19-year-old kid; and while he could play the fuck out of a guitar, his financial skills hadn't yet developed. Still, this behavior was inexplicable to many of us - especially as it had emerged at the last possible moment. We were baffled - and pissed.

So with bags packed, schedules cleared, and our fun about to be stolen from us, the rest of the band (plus the roadies – me, Fleming, The Wolff and a dude named Kellerman) – decided that we were still going to go… somewhere. Even though the actual tour had to be cancelled at the last minute, the adventure would go on. And so on that cold March morning, we piled into our rented minivan and began a quest for fun and daring exploits. Since the tour would have taken us south, we decided to cut the bullshit and head straight for Florida. The events that followed would come to be known collectively as "Florida One."

There was something, uh... distinctive! about being dudes from New Jersey, hurtling aimlessly through the deep South. Maybe it was the green hair, or the tattoos, or the loud mouths. Perhaps it was the fact that we rolled seven deep, or that most of us wrote graffiti everywhere we went. Or that we left most rest stops by lighting a Roman candle in the parking lot and peeling out. Regardless, a directly proportional relationship seemed to emerge: as the locations became more remote, local reaction to our presence became more acute. Yeah, I'd say that "distinctive" is a good word for that.

For the most part, we made the trip to Florida in one shot. There were, of course, a couple of Waffle House stops. And who could resist the famous Route 95 tourist trap known as South of the Border? (Translation: fireworks.) Still, it wasn't long before we hit the Florida state line; an arrival which meant that we'd made it. Sort of.

It was bright morning when we found ourselves at the Florida welcome center. Having now completed the bulk of our journey, a break from 70 miles per hour seemed appropriate. Especially since some of us were beginning to develop that certain madness - the one which can overtake a body after too much van and too many dudes. You just need a rest, you know?

So we stopped, smoked cigarettes, brushed teeth and walked around. And I can only blame the aforementioned van-madness for what happened next. For as I exited the rest stop bathroom, I was strangely transformed. Wearing my dark sunglasses, I flipped the front of my t-shirt over the back of my head. I then hiked the bottoms of my pant legs up, bunching them so that my pants now looked like a bizarre puffy Speedo. It was impossibly stylish.

But the transformation was only complete once I became animated and started jumping around the rest stop like a total idiot. I ran, crept, crab-walked and tip-toed. With my body in a semi-crouching posture and my arms extended out, I resembled some sort of cross between a chimpanzee and the Karate Kid gearing up to throw The Crane. And of course, there were the sounds I made, which were just weird. The most common one was a loud, bird-like, "Ba-DOOOO!" (There was also a soft, cooing, inquisitive "Wa-Tooooh?") And the fan favorite, "KIII-KIII-KIII-KIII-KIII-KIII-KOOOO!"

Yes, the transformation; also known as acting like an asshole. The targets of my mischief were, unforgivably, the other road-weary strangers who milled about the rest stop. And boy, did I ever get right up in some of their faces. Sure, I tried to avoid conveying anything that could be received as aggressive or violent. But my little display nonetheless elicited a fearful response from most innocent bystanders. Usually, people just got the fuck away from me (which is probably what I would have done). Then there were those few who kind of got the joke and just laughed; and then those other few who were totally paralyzed with fear. Overall, it turned out to be an interesting social experiment. Folks' reactions to the whole thing varied a *lot*; except, of course, for the reaction from my crew - who all laughed uproariously at both my behavior and their uncomfortable embarrassment on my behalf. Either Craig or The Wolff subsequently named said act the "Naked Martian Dance," and over the course of countless rest-stops to come, the dance's protagonist – the Naked Martian – would become something of a legend in his own right. Or at least, he's a legend now, since he's here in my book.

Describing the emergence of the Naked Martian is difficult for me, because it *was* me, and I don't really know why or how it happened. Whatever the reason, one thing was clear – I committed to it each and every time. And looking back, the Naked Martian makes perfect sense; or at least it did to me when I was 20. In part, it was a monument to the idea that people should be able to do what they want to do, without fear of being marginalized. In another way, the Naked Martian helped me to express my respect for the value of shock. (To this day, I remain convinced that shock – in its relative, raw subjectivity – is often a good way to jump-start lazy brains.) And of course, let's not forget – I was a 20-year-old kid with nothing better to do than act like an idiot.

So that was the Florida Welcome Center: the Naked Martian fucked with some people, we splashed water on our faces, and we left. Sipping complimentary OJ from paper cups and launching bottle rockets from the moving van, we drove through the morning into mid-day. Gainesville was sort of close and supposedly had a great punk rock scene, so that's where we went. We were down for whatever.

Rounding 22 hours of near-continuous travel, not one of us had enjoyed any meaningful sleep in a long, long time. So it was in a state of near delirium that we finally reached Gainesville early that afternoon. Famished, we stopped at a strip mall pizza place and learned a tough lesson about Floridian pizza. Then someone asked one of the waiters if he could help us find some weed. Amazingly, the guy said yes, and offered his phone number and telling us to call him later. We ate shitty pizza and then relocated to our mobile command center, a.k.a. rented mini van. Pat, P-Nut and Fleming skated the strip mall parking lot, but not for long. We were really, really tired.

Sneaking seven people into one motel room isn't just a cost-effective way to make accommodations affordable for all – it's extremely easy. So we found a Days Inn and made our move. It was all about showers and finding some sleep; bare essentials that go a long way when you started your day a thousand miles back.

And with ten days of playing "Not my town!" ahead of us, we needed all the energy we could muster.

Most of us slept through the late afternoon into the evening. Only as evening became night time did the lot of us began to stir. We'd all recharged enough to go find some adventure. Pat dialed the pizza dude, who said that he would be at a party and that we could meet him there later in order to acquire the aforementioned contraband. Clearly, it was something of a sketchy situation. After all, we were basically going to a house full of strangers to buy an illegal substance. We didn't know anything about the people we'd encounter, or what sort of kid we were *really* dealing with in Pizza Boy. None of us thought twice about any of this.

Luckily, it turned out that we had absolutely nothing to worry about. As a matter of fact, upon our arrival at the party, it became pretty clear that *we* were the sketchiest people around, possibly for miles. Someone made the illicit transaction and the seven of us then went outside to ponder the rest of our night. As we stood there, discussing our plan in the middle of a residential street, a crazy shoeless hippie walked up. He was smoking pot out of a giant glass water pipe. He did a crazy hippie weed dance when he smoked his pot – he'd touch the pipe to his forehead and do the Kid-n-Play dance or something. He was weird, and pretty funny, and I'm sure that at least one of us laughed in his face before we decided to call it a night. As psyched as we were to be in a strange and interesting place, most of us really needed a solid night of sleep. So we went back to the motel, hung out for a while and then deflated. It had been a manic 36 hours.

Like New Brunswick, Gainesville is a college town. So the next day we decided to locate and explore the area around the University of Florida. Knowing that college campuses often help to anchor a town's broader punk and hardcore community, we were eager to find some cool kids and make them into friends. We stopped at every record store, thrift shop and vegetarian-friendly eating establishment we could find.

But for all of our roaming and exploring, we failed to meet any cool people. Sadly, the highlight of the day had been getting the local indie record store to take some records and fanzines on consignment. As evening approached, we began to wonder where we were going to sleep that night. Heading over to the center of the university's campus, our plan was to loiter – and hopefully meet some punk rockers who would offer us a floor. And that's pretty much what happened.

Patty really had no business letting us into her home. She was tiny - even waif-like - and we were seven screaming scumbag strangers from New Jersey who weren't in Florida for any reason other than to hang out. And while all common sense underscores the potential danger in inviting groups of strangers into one's home, Patty didn't care. She walked by us, we started a conversation and within moments we were invited to sleep on her floor.

I suspect that Patty felt comfortable inviting us in for the same reasons we felt comfortable imposing on her – because at some level, we all believed that this was how the world should work. Whether it was punk and hardcore, or plain youthful idealism, we were invoking and enacting a sort of communal trust we hoped more people might consider. Admittedly, it was a simple act – asking a stranger for shelter and receiving it. But within the act itself there was a tacit defiance; the rebuking of a modern society in which, to most folks, the idea of asking a stranger for a place to sleep is absurd.

Whether it was our t-shirts or similar tastes in rock and roll music, many of the legitimate concerns surrounding this otherwise "risky" behavior seemed to fly right out the window. Countless aspects of the modern world have the effect of distancing individuals from other individuals, or pitting them against one another. Implicitly, our shared approach was to say "fuck that noise." In moments like these, *being* punk rock was something much different than *liking* punk rock, or just listening to it. Anyone who was for real just knew – it was more than music. And we could prove it.

Of course, people are people. So when Patty's roommate Aaron first came home and found us all over his house – well, he was more than slightly annoyed. And understandably so. After all, Patty hadn't asked Aaron if it was cool to host a bunch of random anonymous dudes with greasy hair and a mini van. But he came around pretty quickly, either because of all that punk rock mumbo jumbo, or because we were into lots of the same stuff – fireworks, breaking things, punk rock. He loved beer, and so did most of the dudes in our little party. We all got along so well, in fact, that the seven of us wound up staying on Patty and Aaron's floor for three nights. And we painted Gainesville red. There was a party every night, good vegetarian food everywhere and lots of Schlitz in the (novel-to-Jersey-dudes) 32 ounce bottle.

Having been a long-time fan of Gainesville's favorite punk rock sons, Hot Water Music, I was stoked when Aaron's friend Chuck, who happened to be in said band, came down to hang on a couple of those nights. Once again, punk rock was working the way it was "supposed" to – and I was getting a chance to meet and become friends with individuals whose work had genuinely impacted me. It was a wonderful (and accidental) exercise in smashing the notion that people who become well-known for playing music are somehow super-human. I mean, by no means had Hot Water Music achieved the kind of fame to which many of today's bands aspire. But the band had been a touring machine, and were starting to emerge as the institution they'd eventually become in punk and hardcore circles around the world. And here I was, hanging out with, like, the main dude from the band, night after night. And we were becoming friends. It was awesome, and weird.

Gainesville was a *lot* of fun. We set a couch on fire in Patty and Aaron's front yard. We picked televisions from the trash of the Goodwill store around the corner and smashed them to bits. We wrote on everything, everywhere. I called my parents (way back in Marlton) from the back room of a fast-food taco joint, after asking the kid at the counter if I could call my mom who lived down the road. We even saw the immediate aftermath of a minor car accident. The trip had been eventful to say the least. But all that stuff became small potatoes once we met the woman who would come to be known simply as "The Crazy Lady."

Once again, someone in our delegation had asked a Floridian about weed. While Aaron himself didn't know where to find it, he did know someone who knew someone. So Aaron invited all seven of us over to his friend's house, so his friend could call a guy, who would come over to the house to sell weed to Jersey dudes. Yes, it was as awkward as it sounds. So awkward, in fact, that as we waited, the Naked Martian made a surprise entrance from the kitchen. The poor Floridians - they had no fucking idea what was going on. All they knew was that there were seven large male strangers in their house, and one of them was making bird noises and flipping the fuck out.

We continued waiting at said house of ill-repute, where we learned that someone had recently been murdered in one of the upstairs bedrooms. This, of course, made us feel just great. Learn your lessons, people – marijuana is bad news.

The weed guy was taking a while to show up, so I stepped outside for a cigarette and a change of scenery. But only a few moments passed before a white sports car pulled up. Three people got out. The driver was a 20-something man with shaggy hair and a Hawaiian shirt – I don't think he could have been anyone *but* a drug dealer. His girlfriend got out of the passenger seat – she was petite and trashy, and holding a smooth, baseball-sized stone in her hand. She seemed vacant, but somehow still sexy. And then there was her. The fucking Crazy Lady.

She was probably around 35 years old, but looked more like a leathery, pickled 48. Stumbling from the back of the white sports car with a full brandy glass in her hand, she slurred an incoherent statement in my general direction before following the dealer and his girlfriend into the house. All three of them were fucked up. The dealer's girlfriend was clearly on ecstasy, possibly for the first fucking time ever – hence the rock, which she was now pressing to her face. And this older woman? The soon-to-be revealed Crazy Lady? Well, this chick was fucking *wasted*. Not to mention her puffy white shirt and that insane 80s feathered hair action. Shit, a total disaster.

A minute or two passed and I realized that I should probably go inside the house and see what was happening. Which is when the circus came to town.

While weed guy sold his weed, his girlfriend just kind of stood there, smiling and fondling her rock. And the Crazy Lady? She laid right into us. This woman was talking, laughing, yelling, moaning – to everyone in the room, about absolutely nothing. But she had a lot of fucking conviction, let me tell you. As she initially engaged us, we quietly asked one another what the fuck was wrong with her. She definitely wasn't just drunk. She accused everyone of everything – which was hilarious, except for the fact that her posture was becoming increasingly more aggressive with each garbled declaration. Before our eyes, Crazy Lady went through half a dozen mood swings – at one point putting her head in P-Nut's lap, and at another getting so close to Craig that he threatened to punch her in the jaw.

But when Crazy Lady finally pointed at all of us and yelled/ moaned "You're all going to Hell!" – well, this shit was starting to seem straight-up dangerous. Thankfully there was no dramatic climax and the three mystery drug guests left the house; undoubtedly to do more of the great drugs which had made them so charming in the first place. But the Crazy Lady had imprinted herself permanently upon our young minds - and in our photo albums. We even made her pose for a group shot with all seven of us. Life would never be the same.

On the fourth day of our Floridian mania, we decided to stop testing our luck. We said goodbye to Patty and Aaron, who'd now become like family in a way, and we all promised to hang out again. (This promise was kept, by the way, many times over throughout the next few years.) It had been awesome, but we didn't want to wear out our welcome. Plus, we had six or seven more days of adventure to find.

We were on our way out of Gainesville when we stopped at a park to pee and explore the finest in northern Floridian wilderness. Bladders empty, we were about to start moving again when Fleming was compelled to leave Mother Nature with a parting shot. He found a sizeable ant-hill, pushed an M-80 into the top, and lit the fuse. And it blew up, alright – but not before at least one of those doomed little ants got in a good bite on Fleming's finger. Mother Nature can be a motherfucker.

The drive to Daytona wasn't the most comfortable thing for ol' Fleming. It seems that whatever kind of ant had bitten Fleming was especially vengeful, as he became quite ill almost immediately. Of course, this caused him to vomit out of the passenger side window as we first pulled onto the main drag in Daytona. By the time we found a motel, he was sweating bullets and had the chills. Not good.

So we put Fleming in a bed, blasted the air conditioner and rested, wondering at what point we needed to consider the hospital for our sick friend. It was looking grim, especially as time passed and Fleming didn't seem to get better. But after a few hours and a lot of sweat, Fleming did miraculously recover - and almost entirely in a single instant. I myself was relaxing on the motel room floor when he snapped out of his ant fever, celebrating his recovery by running over and putting his balls on my forehead. Everyone – especially Fleming - thought that shit was pretty funny. Strangely, I didn't.

With Fleming back in the saddle it was time once again to play a rousing game of "Not My Town!" What we hadn't anticipated was that Daytona during spring break would be a nightmare. It was like Seaside Heights back in Jersey – un-ironic mullets, barbed wire bicep tats, and airbrushed t-shirts. Worse, we spent most of the next day on the beach, and none of us thought to wear sun-block. This was a huge mistake, but we were too busy hopping into the pools of the beachfront hotels. We'd pose as guests, catch a cool dip, fuck with some people and move on to the next. At the very least, it was something to do. I mean, we *were* in Daytona.

Still, you can't make lemonade out of dog shit – a fact that found us soon exiting Daytona and heading for Tampa, where we didn't fare much better. The first people we saw as we drove into that cursed city were carrying what looked like a dead body into a building; and then there was that hobo, crossing the street and playing air-fiddle. As we came to a stop at the red light, he walked out into the street and approached the driver's side of our van, asking me some kind of question. Although I don't remember what the question was, I do remember hitting the gas and running the red light to get away from his weird ass.

Unable to find anything interesting in Tampa that Saturday night, we headed to Kellerman's grandmother's house; she lived in a gated retirement community just outside of the city. Before our departure from New Jersey she had offered to put us up for a night. We were now quick to take her up. Most of us likely had some level of sun poisoning by this point – which inspired, among other pleasures, an un-fun tournament of the universally beloved Slap Game (a rousing diversion played for thousands of years – it involves being an asshole to your sunburned friends).

But in spite of tender, red skin and subtle nausea, Grandma Kellerman's house was the shit. She was nice, accommodating, and glad to have us. And we were glad to have her and her amenities. Showers, television, and some delicious vegetarian-friendly, grand-motherly home cooking were just what we needed to recharge and tear up more of the south.

With time running out and just a few more days before everyone was due back to the drudgery of work and school, a renewed sense of urgency hit our delegation. Having enjoyed a night of solid and comfortable sleep, we headed back to Gainesville, where our new friends were glad to receive us again. Patty, Aaron and all the other Gainesvillians we'd since befriended were stoked that we'd returned before heading north, so we made the night a blow-out. Patty and Aaron's floor almost felt like home turf that night, and we slept well. The next morning we woke up early and started home.

We stopped in South Carolina for a night, where we stumbled upon a wacky car convention of some sort. South Carolina was also where we watched a pickup truck flying two Confederate flags roll across a beach full of black folks. And we were like, "holy shit!" when we saw a middle-aged black man get up from sitting with his family to run after the Jeep and snatch one of the flags. He snapped the pole across his knee and yelled angrily about the racist bullshit we had all witnessed. We northern boys could barely believe what we were seeing.

As we pushed further north, I got in touch with Chad. Having spoken to him from Grandma Kellerman's house, I knew he'd be at a party in the suburbs of Richmond on a certain night, and it just so happened that the we were set to pass through that particular area of Virginia on the evening of the party. So it was with minimal effort that we stopped at said shindig, where we encountered, amongst many other things, a shower full of dudes, lots of yelling, and drunk people. The party was at someone's parents' very nice house, and the people there sure did seem to be having a heck of a lot of fun. But we only stayed for a short while before setting off on the last few hours of our trip back to New Jersey. Now that we were within 5 hours of New Brunswick, home was pretty much the only thing any of us could think about.

We made it from Richmond to the Garden State line in a criminally short amount of time. The closer we got to home, the more we wanted to get there; and we were now on autopilot, retracing well-worn steps up the New Jersey Turnpike and then, a little past Trenton, grabbing Route 1 North. Except for a short delay in the Princeton area - we had to double back and gather a bunch of our sneakers which had somehow made it out the van window and onto the highway – the wee hours of the morning seemed to peel away quickly. Dawn cracked the darkness as we pulled into our pocket of Middlesex County on that cold March morning. We parted ways, each of us eagerly anticipating a reunion with that old friend, privacy. It was ten amazing days, for sure – but we were super sick of each others' feet.

While Florida One didn't turn out to be The Degenerics' first tour, it sure had been something to remember. Sure, from a band perspective, time and resources were definitely lost. But I guarantee that not one of us who were there would take it back for anything. It was, in the end, a life-changing experience for the seven of us; probably, at least in part, for the same reasons that sorority sisters will always treasure that spring break in Cozumel – and that's okay. That's like coming of age and shit – just done our own punk rock kind of way. And anyway, it's not like The Degenerics wouldn't have another chance to tour. Hell, they'd made so many friends along the way that once the band came through for real, folks would be waiting with baited breath.

Exploits like these helped define the dedication and faith that surrounded both The Degenerics and Worthless. Before long, both bands assumed a mantle of vague and accidental leadership; at least within our little corner of the universe/New Jersey punk scene. They played constantly and often together; they also released records around the same time, and before most of their friends' bands. With the Masonic Temple now consistently in play, a new momentum was clearly erupting. Of course, other bands and people were essential in helping to compose that momentum, like S.O.V. and Crawford's band Stormshadow (featuring red-headed Sue on the axe of fire and Jamie from instil on drums). But at least for a short while, The Degenerics and Worthless seemed to be at the center of it all.

What I found most interesting was the way in which the two bands were simultaneously similar and distinct; how they represented different aspects of the same aesthetic. The Degenerics were pissed and furious, while Worthless played silly and fun; aggression opposite anthems. Punk rock yin, punk rock yang. Of course, it's more likely that the "vast" difference I detected between The Degenerics and Worthless revealed how myopic my vision was at the time; it's easy to argue that The Degenerics and Worthless were largely identical. Like, would an alien from another planet even be able to tell the two bands apart? Probably not. But I was having a lot of fun - in spite of analyses, observations and debates. Yes, it was all very fun.

Still, I felt that little pinch at the back of my neck – the gnawing, irresistible desire to have my own band. This music, its messages, and the people and culture of hardcore and punk had given me so much, and I felt a drive and responsibility to give something back. Sure, by this point, I'd done plenty with *Aneurysm* – at least, enough for it to be qualified as a "legitimate" or "substantial" contribution. But I was sick of postulating about songs and offering opinions of bands or records. Not to mention that attempts like Redshift and the Lost Boys had only intensified my drive to find the right situation. I was prepared to look high and low. And since my house was constantly overrun with people, I had a good place to start.

My first attempt in this renewed mission was a gathering that included myself, Little Pedro, Rory the Skinhead, a Skinhead girl named Alexa who played bass in her bra, and a drummer whose name escapes me but who was a tool. Packed into the sweltering attic of 62 Guilden Street, we tried to write some music. While the whole experience was pretty much shit, my prior experience with bands had made it so that such mediocrity was really just par for the course. Maybe this was my permanent reality – that trying to be in a band would always feel like walking through waist-high molasses in January.

For all of my efforts, I was starting to become discouraged when the first piece of my band puzzle was to be found, ironically, right under my nose. In the end, it was as easy as a casual conversation. P-Nut and I were driving around late one night listening to Sunny

Day Real Estate's *Diary*, when I mentioned how serious I was about starting something. Maybe it would even sound like Sunny Day Real Estate, I mused. And just like that, P-Nut said that he'd be down to play drums if I could get something together. To this day, I have no idea why I hadn't previously considered asking him to play music with me, especially since we had become such close friends. Whatever the reason, I now had an awesome drummer for the band of my dreams.

And plus, there was Fanshen.

The Wolff wanted to play music again and decided to put together a new version of K.G.B. And although Pat and Frank were focused on (and possibly obsessed with) The Degenerics, The Wolff convinced them to play with him in this new band - Pat on guitar, Frank on drums. The Wolff, of course, would reprise his role of maniacal frontman. And on the bass, either out of pity or stupidity... Ronen Kauffman!

Of course, I had never played a bass before in my life. But this was punk rock, so it wasn't supposed to matter. I took the few things I knew about guitar (I'd gotten *slightly* better since trying out for Worthless), applied them to my new career as a bassist, and was ready to kick ass. We began to write and practice our fast, angry songs; and for a while it seemed like I might be able to bullshit my way through being a bass player. At the very least, I was having fun playing fast, angry music with my friends.

I suggested calling the band "We've Got A Bomb," but it was Fleming who ultimately named the band *Fanshen* - he'd recently read a book of that name, about revolution in a rural Chinese village throughout the 1940s and '50s. In Chinese, "fanshen" is really two words meaning literally "to turn over." In the midst of violence and poverty, the embroiled Chinese peasantry interpreted this as a slogan for their struggle; the metaphor of "turning over" became the promise of a new dawn for the people, if they worked hard. Fleming explained all of this to us; it was all right up The Wolff's alley, and so that was that.

Manic thrashy songs? Check. Insane front man with the soul of a poet? Check. Cool symbolic-slash-political name? Check.

But none of that made me a decent bass player. Not even a little bit.

Our first performance in front of living people was in my kitchen at 52 Wyckoff Street – and we were *way* out of our league. I'm pretty sure that I didn't hit one note correctly in the four songs we played. It's even possible I didn't hit any notes at all.

After such a revealing debut, I was no longer able to hide my gross inadequacies when it came to playing the bass. But the other dudes in Fanshen behaved as good friends do, saying that I'd catch on quickly, not to be discouraged, and so on. Still, I didn't show much improvement after that first show and I knew that the guys in Fanshen would eventually want to play real shows and have a real bass player. Yet even with the knowledge that my day would have to come, I still had a good time. Maybe it was because I wanted the fun to last. Maybe it was because I was subconsciously deluded, convinced that I'd somehow become a bassist and travel a road I never imagined. Or maybe it was because I was simultaneously in the process of putting *my* band together. My *real* band.

Still, this was a really difficult task. After all, it wasn't as if I had written a bunch of songs and just needed some dudes to play them. To the contrary. By this point, I'd proven a couple of times that such an eventuality was not possible. With singing now the only thing I could do in a band without embarrassing myself (or others), my burden became clear; if I wanted to play music, I'd have to find people who played instruments. And with so little musical experience under my belt, it seemed like a hard sell to prospective collaborators. Perhaps the only ace I had was that P-Nut was in place to play drums. P-Nut was, after all, a powerful and impressive drummer. So at the very least, I could guarantee potential band mates that *he* didn't suck.

Still, the backbone of the whole idea – the melodies, the rhythms, the songs themselves – well, that stuff was all completely up in the air. All I knew was that I didn't want to play ska.

For all the ambiguity I faced in terms of what was to come musically, the ideas that underpinned the whole experience for me were becoming more distinct by the day. All around me, bands were (usually unknowingly) piecing together the personal and the political, and those were the ones after which I began to model my own work. And while I couldn't channel that spirit through a guitar, I could definitely do so with words and an aesthetic that clearly reflected my reasons for playing music in the first place. I looked to those bands that had exacted the most influence on me at the time – standbys, like Operation Ivy and Minor Threat, as well as acts with more proximity, like Four Walls Falling, Avail and even Endeavor. To me, the only "real" bands were ones that reflected realism, honesty, a genuineness of expression and a certain clever rebellion. Sounding good was important to me, but not as important as what I interpreted as being "real."

I didn't know Adolfo, but I knew *of* him. He was from the same corner of Jersey as Zak, who had mentioned his name a few times. Adolfo played in a band called Sky Falls Down with my friend Casey, a fellow zine nerd I met at the *Daily Targum*. Sky Falls Down was something of a post-core emo metal band or whatever; really awesome, and totally unique. (Casey later went on to play in the influential band You and I, and later in

Philadelphia's Hot Cross.) So yeah, Adolfo was a bass player, and happened to wind up in one of my classes that spring. It was good timing, so I made my move.

The timing turned out to be better than I expected, because Sky Falls Down was apparently in its death rattle. Additionally, Adolfo and one of the guitarists from Sky Falls Down – a guy named Chris Byrnes – had been working on a separate band called Fire Lotus Society, which had also been experiencing some trouble. I told him that I was looking to sing and that I could bring a great drummer with me. Adolfo expressed interest and said that he could probably bring Byrnes along to check us out. We exchanged phone numbers, and within a day or two had set up a meeting. This was an exciting development.

It was early May of 1997 when the four of us – myself, P-Nut, Adolfo and Byrnes – first played together in the basement of a house on Plum Street. Predictably, the first moments were sort of awkward and delicate. We were, after all, only slightly more than two pairs of strangers. But we'd convened with a common cause – and while I can not attest to why the other guys were there, I knew that I was seeking much more than just a rock band. I wanted collaboration and friendship. I wanted to evoke something soulful and mighty. And I wanted to do right by the music that had done so much for me.

Byrnes had come ready to present the material he'd written, but what we really needed that day was to break musical bread together. And since the only song we all knew how to play was "Burning Fight" by seminal California hardcore band Inside Out, that became our very first jam. We certainly didn't sound perfect, but the energy emanating from that basement held our collective attention. It was fun, and it was loud, and we all got along like enthusiastic peas and carrots.

After going through "Burning Fight" a few times, Byrnes and

Adolfo ran through some Fire Lotus Society material with P-Nut. It was loud and heavy, but melodic; it also had a rapid tempo. There were some hooks in there, and some crunchy parts, and it was definitely not radio rock. (At least, not back then.)

Not having heard any of their material beforehand, I was both impressed and relieved.

Byrnes played dutifully. He apparently had the prerequisite songwriting skills, as well as a particular intensity that made him come off as some sort of guitar Godzilla. Not to mention that he was stacked head-to-toe in gigantic muscles. Other than music, most of Byrnes' time was spent studying nutrition in college and lifting weights. The dude loved Leeway and Queensryche. He was clearly awesome.

Adolfo used his fingers instead of a pick. His guitar strap was shortened so that his bass rested somewhat high on his lean frame. At times this looked sort of nerdy, but it was the only way he was able to pull off the dense, notey bass lines he played when accompanying Byrnes. Adolfo played organically, getting by mostly on feel; stylistically, the contrast he offered to Brynes' technical precision was quite complimentary.

P-Nut listened, slowly dropping in simple beats until his instincts took over – at which point the drumming machine inside of him did the rest. Within moments, the three of them had worked out a number of parts, linked a couple of them, and just like that – songs! Well, maybe not songs, but something with promise.

We agreed to meet again and it soon became pretty clear that we all recognized some potential. By the third or fourth practice, I began laying down vocals, and suddenly we were a band.

I stole the name try.fail.try from Chad. He had recently told me that he'd come up with it as a name for a positive hardcore band after reading the well-known poem "Autobiography in Five Short Chapters" by Portia Nelson:

Autobiography In Five Short Chapters

Chapter I

I walk down the street.
There is a deep hole in the sidewalk.
I fall in.
I am lost ---- I am helpless ---- it isn't my fault. . . . .
It takes forever to find a way out.

Chapter II

I walk down the same street.
There is a deep hole in the sidewalk.
I pretend I don't see it.
I fall in again.
I can't believe I am in the same place ---- but it isn't my fault. . . .
It still takes a long time to get out.

Chapter III

I walk down the same street.
There is a deep hole in the sidewalk.
I see it is there.
I still fall in . . . . It is a habit.
My eyes are open.
I know where I am.
It is my fault.
I get out immediately.

Chapter IV

I walk down the same street.
There is a deep hole in the sidewalk.
I walk around it.

Chapter V

I walk down another street.

Given the ideas I was hoping to pour into my new band – hopefully, my "dream" band - the name try.fail.try seemed perfect. It sounded *human*, just as I knew the tone of my band had to be. I offered the name up to my new band mates and they favored it unanimously. Now all I had to do was explain to Chad that I'd stolen his idea. Though he was slightly pissed at first, he got over it. Anyway, it wasn't like Chad was about to use the name for anything. He was busy playing around the D.C. scene with his own chaotic, screamy band, Amalgamation (which incidentally included one dude who went on to be in The Rapture).

So try.fail.try was ours and things progressed quickly. Byrnes and Adolfo had lots of good material, P-Nut worked quickly, and my lyrics were ready to go. The process of crafting our new baby had begun, and it was exciting. Not to mention that my media obsession was shifting and mutating. If before I'd felt that *Aneurysm* wasn't enough to keep me happy, now the fanzine had become little more than a chore; with its rapid expansion, the constant work of keeping up to date with everything had even become more than I could handle on my own. And if I'd been losing my patience with traditional journalism, finally having a band caused me to just plain check out. I even stepped down from all of my editorial duties at *Targum*, stopped writing all together, and got a job designing ads in the paper's production office.

Commonly known as "Pro," Targum Productions was where the newspaper and other publications were designed and produced nearly around the clock - a totally separate facility from the editorial office of the newspaper, with a completely different culture. And because of its access to said production tools, this place was an employment magnet for punk and hardcore types. (It probably still is.) You couldn't have Photoshop or QuarkXpress in 1996 without expecting to do at least one late-night favor for a hardcore kid. I mean, shit - the layout in Deadguy's classic *Fixation on a Coworker* had been done at Pro.

My junior year of college ended and suddenly everyone I knew was facing June 1 – the first/last day of many New Brunswick leases. While 52 Wyckoff Street had been lots of fun, its number was clearly up. We'd discovered an inversely proportional relationship between the number of holes in the walls and our landlord's disposition – the more holes, the more the guy hated us. And in the end (with a 1-year total of 47 holes), he hated us a lot. He hated us so much that he even got mad when Tweety had a particularly handy friend come over to patch up all the holes, including one the size of a large man's rear end, and another which housed the remains of a half-eaten Fat Cat sandwich placed there weeks prior . A little sheetrock, a little spackle, and bam! Instant return of our security deposit. Yeah, the landlord fucking hated us.

Room mate Andy decided he'd had enough. I guess he just hadn't expected that Wyckoff Street would really be *that* punk rock.

"Nick" Nicoletti left the house halfway through the year and was subsequently replaced by Annie. So the four of us – Crawford, Tweety, Annie and I – decided to relocate as a group. We brought Fid in to replace Andy, and agreed on our only criteria for our next dwelling – that we would each get our own room, with no thru-traffic. It was a tall order – an affordable 5-bedroom apartment in New Brunswick, in a neighborhood that wasn't *too* shady.

But I knew of a place across town, right down the block from Tweety's old apartment at 220 Hamilton. It was then being inhabited by a couple of dudes from Endeavor and some other kids.

And while "run down" would have been an extremely generous description, we nonetheless saw this place as an affordable way to satisfy our agreed upon criteria. Without a whole lot of thought, we moved into the apartment above the flower shop, at 224 Hamilton Street.

Dammit.

Five – 1997-1998: The Chateau Ghetto

224 Hamilton was huge, but it was disgusting. Years of neglect and numerous punk rock inhabitants had left it in an almost unfathomable state of filth and dilapidation. Nowhere in the apartment was this any more apparent than in the kitchen; from ancient, peeling floor tiles to old steel cabinets spray-painted a dull, gritty red (you could easily imagine finding identical ones in an old Soviet army barracks) – well, let's just say that the place was less than inviting.

In three of the bedrooms were enormous lofts constructed years earlier by some of the Bouncing Souls, also previous tenants. The lofts were actually pretty awesome; but while they helped to capitalize on the largesse of the apartment, they still somehow seemed to contribute to the overall disaster of the place.

There was the area known affectionately as the "Forbidden Room." Our new landlord explained that it wasn't safe to enter this huge, elaborate bathroom because large sections of the floor had gone missing – so that walking into the room might have sent one crashing through the ceiling of the flower shop below. At some point in its abandonment, the walls of the room had been "painted" with brown and green streaks; the kind of interior decorating that easily could have been the result of a prior tenant's drunken adventure. After all, imagine having such a forbidden and literally dangerous place located directly in the center of one's own apartment. Under certain circumstances, it would be totally irresistible. And though upon first glance the Forbidden Room was like something out of a horror movie, in the context of the rest of the place it couldn't have been more perfect.

And yet, 224 Hamilton's general state of disgusting disrepair wasn't enough to sway the five of us from thinking that it could be considered home. Instead, what we saw was a huge place with plenty of privacy for all. We saw a landlord who seemed incredibly laid back – a conclusion based not only on accounts from previous tenants, but also on the condition of the apartment. We saw a functional space that met our needs, where every one of us could have our own bedroom. And - perhaps most importantly - we saw an affordable monthly rent check.

One thing we didn't see was the roach problem. It was insane.

They were everywhere. And I don't just mean, like, in every room. They were in the fucking refrigerator, the cabinets, the damned bathtub. It was like that terrible movie, *Joe's Apartment* – you'd turn the kitchen light on in the middle of the night and see the bastards scatter to the perimeter - under the stove, the fridge, the radiator. It was like watching a brown carpet dissolve in three seconds. By day three of our lease we had enough and demanded that the place be fumigated. Squalor was one thing. Squalor with creepy, filthy, huge brown bugs everywhere was something totally different.

The fumigation required us to stay out of the apartment for 24 hours or so; a small and temporary inconvenience, considering what we were getting in exchange. Luckily, it was easy for me to find a place to crash for the night. Fleming had just moved into an apartment located right across Hamilton Street, on the opposite corner of mine. Having realized this incredibly fortunate coincidence prior to moving in, we'd already declared mutual dominion over the intersection, which among other things meant that I could sleep on his couch.

While it certainly wasn't a palace, 224 Hamilton Street (newly-christened as the "Chateau Ghetto") was perfect for most of us who lived there; a spacious DIY workshop with plenty of space for doing cut-and-paste layouts or bagging up seven inches. And that's a lot of what would define the year we'd spend living in that shit hole - glue sticks, scissors, silk screens and Kinko's copy cards. We were, after all, a busy group of people. Tweety had his band and his radio show. Fid was always playing guitar. Crawford had Stormshadow and his zine, *Tear Down Babylon*. And I'd just put out the first Worthless 7" while working on what I'd decided would be the last issue of *Aneurysm*. And of course, now there was try.fail.try.

Summer went into full swing, and boy did it ever. Between my place and Fleming's, it was often a mob scene, and it was usually pretty great - even during some of our least dignified moments, both individually and collectively. I went to shows, poisoned my body, messed with some girls, had fun and hung out. It was self-defense. My senior year was upon me and the imminent end of college life - my seemingly perfect escape from reality - loomed in the distance like a dark cloud of compromise and adulthood. My politics, my personality, and life in general all felt like they were becoming more intense. Maybe I was trying to prepare for the uncertainty of the future. Or maybe I was just being defensive. Either way, I had a year and I was going to make it count. It was my pledge.

But despite any such bravado, that July I turned 21 to little fanfare. By this point, I'd spent a bunch of birthdays being glum and effacing; so much so that it had become sadly natural for me to become a miserable hermit in the days leading up to and including said birthday. Really, it was some fairly typical growing up stuff – a perfectly normal reaction to standing on the precipice of anything; an annual "These Are the Ways You Could Have

Been Better" sermon which I gave to myself, year after year. So while I pledged to make this the year of taking everything to the next level, my first few steps looked pretty much like ones I'd taken many times before.

As far as everything else, the rest of the summer was status quo – bands, shows and general punk rock wackiness. There were some stand-out moments, of course – like when You and I rocked the Masonic Temple so hard that Justin busted open his head; or the night I saw ball lightning. Or how windy it was that August. But to me the summer seemed to race by, as if it was eager to make room for autumn; like it was tired of being the summer itself. And then, just like that, the fall semester of 1997 was in sight. The air cooled, the antics subsided (slightly), and all of a sudden my last year of college was about to begin.

Whereas some might have dreaded the new marking period, I now lusted after it. I was in deep love with my studies; I'm talking hot brain on book action. So much so that I habitually tried to turn everything I saw into a target for intellectual deconstruction, and then (most likely) ridicule. I extended this charming spirit into almost every area of my waking life, allowing me to take the act of being opinionated to entirely new levels - especially when it came to music. As far as I was concerned, the world was fucked and hardcore punk attracted some of the only worthwhile people to be found. Other subcultures were shit, and mine was the best one. True, "the scene" didn't always seem to fulfill the promise I projected upon it. But I saw real movement and potential. The power of mosh compelled me. It was wholly obnoxious, and awesome.

I'd be put into check for this sort of absolutism by falling in love with a raver. And hey, funny fact about me at age 21 – I thought ravers were complete assholes.

I'd never actually been in love. Sure, I'd had my share of *relations*, if you catch my drift - but no love. I was, of course, too much of a self-absorbed douchebag to understand the nuances of sacrifice and sharing that define a healthy relationship. Like everything else for me at that time, my concepts of "girlfriend" and "relationship" were in a state of flux, resulting from changes taking place in how I saw myself, *in* the world. This meant that I was thinking seriously about what kind of person I wanted to be, and thinking seriously about the things I hated, and thinking seriously about the things I loved. I was hungry for opportunities to learn, grow and change.

Susanna was smart, with big green eyes and a wicked smile. She and I first met in class the previous year and had wound up partially or entirely naked on a couple of very random occasions following that first meeting. But while we shared a definite physical chemistry, plenty of things about the girl pissed me off; perhaps none more than her taste in music. Susanna loved techno and house, which to me was escapist idiot music that celebrated some of humankind's most embarrassing behavior. In fact, dance music on the whole was antithetical to the supposedly more purposeful music I loved; and to reiterate, at the time I occasionally expressed my opinions so strongly that my head would sometimes accidentally slip up into my own ass. Nonetheless, at this stage in my journey ravers were cowardly, selfish hedonists who were doing nothing to set right the injustices of the world. Maybe they didn't see the mediocrity underpinning their tastes and lifestyle, but I did. So beyond touching her boobs, I was never really interested in Susanna as a girlfriend. In fact, I kind of hated her. She was, after all, a fucking raver.

So when she wound up in one of my classes that fall, I instantly found her irritating. To make things even worse, she kept bothering me. But while I first tried to remain intensely disinterested, Susanna was back at my apartment within a week.

This time, though, it was something more than a hook-up; and within a few short days it was clear – despite the techno music, something dramatic and intense was happening between us. Somehow, Susanna and I had fallen in love. Yes, just like that.

Fid had to move out. Frank was 19 years old and ready to leave home, so he took Fid's room.And as the semester hit its stride, so did everything else. Suddenly, I was a senior in college with a beautiful girlfriend and a "sick" hardcore band about to make its debut. It was a far cry from the senior year I'd had four years prior, which was a good thing. Finally, I was able to feel as if I'd really done something for myself, having decided what I *didn't* want to be when I grew up; having made the best choices I could relative to what kind of person I wanted to be in life. I felt confident. I felt good.

Not that I'd experienced too much difficulty with feeling good before this point. On the contrary, I'd always been a fairly affable kid. I liked fun and music, the beach and going to the movies with my friends. I wasn't good at sports and I was not 'popular', but for the most part I always had at least a few pals and desired their company. Yet until punk and hardcore emerged as my lens, I didn't see that most of my time was spent on directionless crap. Underneath the surface, I'd long sensed that the world had its problems and that, in some way, I stood in opposition to those problems. Justice and fairness always felt important to me, most likely because I was reared in part by the spectre of one of history's most horrific crimes against humanity. But being a kid from the suburbs, lost in tract housing and pep rallies – well, I didn't have a way to focus my suspicions and resentments. Not until punk rock.

Now, just a few short years later, I'd become a totally different human, *being*. College and the world at large seemed to be full of people whose lives were being lived for them, by the world

– but not me. My life was mine, and that was exciting. Needless to say, the idea of living life "as one pleases" is kind of silly; no one can truly live outside the bounds of society, because the whole of human civilization includes each and every corner we carve. Even the most provocative rebels are, by their very own existence, bound to the establishment against which they somehow rail. Who is the artist without an audience, or the audience without art?

Looking back on those early years, it now seemed clear to me why hardcore punk had been my choice. Sports, Dungeons & Dragons, school – none of them had offered the freedom and opportunity of punk and hardcore. Nothing did. How else could kids like me feel like they belonged in this fucked up world, unless we were honest about how we felt and dedicated to singing or screaming about it? I saw a veritable cornucopia of solidarity and well-deserved validation. True, such a highly idealized vision of punk rock was never and likely will never be the true face of hardcore culture. But in all of the disagreements about what it *really* means to be 'punk' or 'hardcore', one maxim seems to weather most philosophical storms – that is, that punk or hardcore is what you make of it for yourself. For me, it was a way to speak out, a way to be creative, and a way to live in disciplined harmony with my heart and mind. Hardcore punk led me to adventure and it helped me to feel good about myself when I was pissed or depressed by the sick, sad world all around me.

With my first real girlfriend, my first real band, and more friends than I'd ever had in my entire life, the work of existing was taking on a whole new sensation. Maybe it was love, or maybe it was punk rock, or maybe it was just the chemicals that pump through your brain until you're 24. Whatever it was, life felt crazy - and I liked it.

Push soon came to shove with Fanshen. Essentially, I was relieved; there were no hard feelings, of course, and since try.fail. try was trying to get serious it was really a blessing in disguise. Craig and The Wolff booked a show at the Masonic Temple, which would be the first proper show for Fanshen, and my last with the band. Our set was about eight minutes long and I sucked worse than ever, but it didn't matter to me.

That was because the next band on the bill was try.fail.try. Although we only had four songs to play that day of our first show, we didn't suck – which was pretty much all I could have asked for. And while I'd sung in a few bands by this point, this was a distinctively different experience. And it felt great.

I had a very specific plan in mind for try.fail.try. To me, the world of punk and hardcore was a trading floor in the marketplace of ideas. And the bands I admired most - the ones who seemed to have a genuine reverence for the power of music - often put big ideas way out in front. To me, being outspoken and doing it creatively was the ultimate union of art and function; and this was the guiding principle with which I was crafting the identity of try.fail.try.

At that first show, I handed out photocopied lyric sheets to the people in the crowd before we played. I was adamant that the ideas contained in the lyrics play a big part in framing the band. Early on I imposed internal conditions on how try.fail.try would operate. Though the conditions were largely symbolic, I placed a great deal of importance on them. The rules were simply that 1) we would only play all-ages shows; and 2) we would never play a show that cost more than $5. While that second rule fell by the wayside soon enough, the band's relationship with money (a.k.a. "El Diablo") continued to concern me. It had to be right out in front that try.fail.try was not interested in cash, except maybe in discussing it academically. Our motivation was supposedly supplied by intrinsic benefits much more valuable than any currency.

We played our second show on Halloween, at the Stelton Recreation Center in Edison. Craig got us on the show, which included a diverse group of local bands from the greater Middlesex County area. There was The Degenerics, of course, as well as Handful of Dust, a goth-metal band for which P-Nut was currently also playing. Tweety and the Heidnik Stews were on the bill, as was Feint 13, a metal-hardcore band featuring the infamous New Jersey mosh pit one-man wrecking crew named Fat Pat.

Our set was once again short but it was decidedly better than the previous one. Our repertoire now had six songs and we could competently play almost all of them. This was also a much more exciting show, with a decent sound system and a lot of kids we didn't know – some of whom even threw a couple of spin kicks for us. And since it was Halloween, people were feeling extra festive. Even try.fail.try wore costumes. Wearing all black, we painted our faces yellow and black to resemble the "happy face" image. Then we spattered small amounts of red to resemble dripping or sprayed blood; imagery lifted from the graphic novel *Watchmen* by Alan Moore. And we had stickers and patches for the show, which kids actually wanted. The whole evening was a lot of fun and was a shot of morale for the band.

And while it all felt great, I was still leery of losing perspective; the message always needed to supercede the medium. In other words, I didn't want rock and roll and its back-catalog of failures to take precedent over the values of hardcore punk. To this end, I didn't want to get wrapped up in big dreams and "what-ifs" when it came to my relationship with music. At its most vital and important level, my being in a band was about a moment, an instant of connection between people through an arrangement of sounds. It was certainly not about record sales, merchandise, money, or being a rock star – tiny, modern blips in the greater story of music throughout human civilization. So I kept my goals at a minimum when it came to my band's interactions with the material world. I pretty much only dealt with one goal at a time, the first of which was to play a show. By now we'd done that twice, so we needed a new goal – and that was to make a recording, for the sake of posterity, at the very least.

In the mean time, vibrant, creative, productive people seemed to be everywhere. And while most of the kids I knew arguably had plenty in common with one another, styles and sounds (a.k.a. respective interpretations of the hardcore punk aesthetic) were often drastically different from one individual to the next; at least, within the restrictive genus of punk. But there was often an intangible solidarity in these differences, and nowhere was this more apparent than at shows, which were getting better and better.

Take that November, for example, when a high school kid from East Brunswick named Elliot had planned a Masonic Temple matinee featuring Fanshen, Stormshadow, Autamaton, Worthless and The Degenerics. All the bands shredded that day - but two of them just plain killed everyone.

The Degenerics' set that day was positively explosive; a glimpse of the powerhouse that they were quickly becoming. Both in terms of how they played and crowd reaction, it was an overwhelming and intense event - one of those sets after which you catch the eye of another fan and simply shake your head from side to side, wondering how what just happened was even possible.

Just as The Degenerics had blown the doors off the place, Worthless followed with what was easily the best set I'd ever seen them play. Scott's brother Steve had recently joined, which was something of a coup for Worthless. Steve came from a well-known experimental hardcore band called Standpoint and was a notoriously awesome drummer. With Zak and Steve now leading the band in a more focused and enjoyable direction, a Worthless show had become a reliably good time, with plenty of kids starting to catch on. At this show, the crowd had positioned itself right up front of the band, and we sang along loudly as Worthless plowed through one anthem after another. A few songs in, someone launched a flurry of confetti into the air – the surprise of which thrust me into a dream-like state. It was a sensation similar to the one I'd felt upon first listening to that record on my bedroom floor back in Marlton. Right there in the middle of Worthless' set, pressed up against my friends and immersed in voices, time appeared to slow down; the lights suddenly seemed brighter and the air more vibrant. It was dream-like and euphoric. Singing at the top of my lungs and in unison with my friends, my heart pounded in my chest - with love for my friends, the music we shared, and this way in which we claimed space for ourselves in a world full of compromise. The room and the moment pulsed.

Truly, it was amazing to know that my best friends had written my favorite songs. And the differences between all the bands that played that day underscored a crucial principle within our small community of creative, disillusioned, funny outcasts: that having different interpretations of the same thing is a good thing. Just like in nature, diversity is good for art, expression and the evolution of human thought and consciousness. Diversity is essential.

A general recognition of this spawned the idea of a compilation 7" record, showcasing some of the different sounds and ideas New Brunswick had to offer. Craig came up with the name *Right to Assemble* and suggested that we put the record out collectively, without the involvement of a record label. This approach made perfect sense given the collectivist culture of our little enclave. So Craig, The Wolff, Zak and I managed the project, choosing the bands we thought best suited to the record. *Right to Assemble, Volume One* would include try.fail.try, The Degenerics, Worthless, Fanshen, Stormshadow and Heidnik Stew.

Indirectly, the conception of *Right To Assemble* became a landmark event for try.fail.try, because it pushed us into achieving the aforementioned goal of making a recording. We picked the song we felt would be easiest to record – a freight train called "For Freedom" -and decided to record with a guy named Dave Meyer, who had a modest studio in northern Jersey called Third Studio from the Sun. Dave had done a decent job for some of our friends' bands and he was affordable, so we pooled our cash and booked the time.

Admittedly, I was a little nervous. I'd never recorded my vocals in a proper studio setting before and I was terrified that a high-fidelity recording of my voice might reveal something unexpectedly shitty. Not to mention that because we were on such limited time and money, there wouldn't be time for lots of takes. I'm pretty sure all of us in the band were pleasantly surprised (and relieved) when my vocals didn't take too long and turned out okay. Not like I can say the same for Adolfo and his bass parts, but hey, shit happens.

Although we'd played a number of local shows by this point, no one really knew what try.fail.try sounded like until we recorded "For Freedom." Thankfully, what emerged from that first real studio experience was a recording I still enjoy. It was loud, and pissed, and purposed. The sound was kind of raw, but not bad for the money, and we were proud of the song; our friends seemed to be proud of us, too. Not to mention that as a band we'd set and accomplished another goal, which was invigorating. On a personal level, I was ecstatic. I had recorded a real song with my own band for a record that people were actually going to buy and hear. All the other guys in the band had already done that, but not me. So it was a nice feeling and I felt a sensation of once again coming full circle. Not to mention that we'd done it all ourselves; as a unit, try.fail.try was really starting to thrive.

Of course, working collectively can have its rough spots and the four of us who managed the production of *Right to Assemble* encountered plenty of them as we worked to get the project done. But despite a few arguments, the comp came out. And although a debacle involving the promotion of the record release show wound up permanently ending our residency at the Masonic Temple - end of an era, blah, blah - early that March we had a record release show in the basement of Demarest Hall. All six *Right to Assemble* bands played to a crowd of probably 150 people, including band members - a modest turnout by some standards, but not bad for our little project.

At the time, there was a lot of punk and hardcore related stuff in New Brunswick, and by no means had we hoped to release a definitive document that captured the entire picture. We were just friends with something cool going on, and we were psyched to celebrate it, and to push it forward. For us, there was a statement in having the jazz-punk influenced Stormshadow on the same slab of vinyl as anthemic Worthless or manic Fanshen. Bands – even the ones in the so-called 'punk' scene – often seem to craft their music with trends in mind, capitalizing on the most popular style of any given moment. Our common drive was the opposite – to sound distinct from and unlike one another. Sure, there's a bitch of a contradiction in the notion of striving collectively for uniqueness; but nonetheless this was the culture of our community, and *Right to Assemble, Volume One* epitomized this.

Beyond sonic diversity, we felt it critical that the compilation be more than just an array of captured sounds. The booklet insert, for example, included step-by-step instructions on how to put out a 7" record, complete with costs, manufacturers' phone numbers, and tips on distribution. *Right to Assemble* wasn't intended simply as a cool, classic record meant to promote an eclectic group of punk rockers; it was a concrete way to share ideas, resources, and motivation – and hopefully, to inspire others to go off and make their own noise.

Depending on how you look at things, the hard work behind the compilation paid off. *Maximum RockandRoll*'s reviewer loved it, and kids throughout Jersey bought copies like hotcakes. With six bands selling them and local record stores on board, it wasn't long before *Right to Assemble, Volume One* went into a second pressing. And as the first recorded release from try.fail.try, this little DIY compilation was putting my band on all kinds of new radars, to a mostly positive response. It wasn't long before try.fail.try realized that we'd have to record again, and soon.

Of course, when it rains it pours. As try.fail.try was shifting into the next gear, Dan called me to talk about the new band he was forming after the recent breakup of Lifetime. He had a fast, melodic hardcore punk band in mind, and was wondering if I'd be interested in trying out to be the singer. I was, of course, immediately flattered when I learned that my recommendation had come from Lifetime's vocalist, Ari, who had seen me play with Redshift earlier that year at Cheap Thrills, then his place of employment. And I was psyched that an outside observer with legitimate band experience – and someone I admired artistically - thought that I was at least passable.

Dan sent me a cassette with some rough recordings of a few songs. I was of course stoked at the possibility of doing this band, but I couldn't escape the fact that the material was much more melodic than what I was interested in playing. Since arriving in New Brunswick, I had been exposed to one new thing after another, causing my tastes to widen and shift rapidly. So while Yemin's crisp breakdowns and bright hooks were great, they just didn't gel with where my head was at the time. More and more, my interest shifted toward heavier, angrier material, which was reflected in the solid foundation I'd begun to lay with Byrnes, P-Nut and Adolfo. Choosing to stick with try.fail.try, I passed on my opportunity to try out for the band that would soon become known as Kid Dynamite.

It wasn't that I stopped liking the catchier punk music that had filled me up for so many years. All of the influences I heard on that early Kid Dynamite demo, from Gorilla Biscuits to 7 Seconds, were all still front and center in my relationship with hardcore punk. But all the different things to which I'd now been exposed had exacted their unavoidable influence upon me. Layers of judgment and/or ignorance that I didn't even know I had were now peeling away. From grind to crust to Oi! to d-beat to math metal and youth crew to a little something called "tough-guy chug-chug," the range of possibilities for punk rock in my mind was limitless.

Throughout my years of interest in this stuff, I cycled through a number of opinions on what it *really* meant to "be" hardcore or punk. But the breadth of musical and aesthetic possibilities had turned my focus to a new fixation – the confusing division that seemed to separate people from one another within the punk or hardcore scene itself; discord between people who, at least on the surface, seemed to have so much in common. From Skinheads to emo kids, from NYHC to youth crew to crust to Krishna-core, I wondered about the ambiguous, common thread binding us all to one another. Despite punk's dramatic splintering, all interpretations were valid in their claims to a common pedigree. No matter how it was evoked, a central theme of reaction and expression cut across all the sub-scenes and cliques.

To this end, I was now well aware that punk – which I once had perceived as an emotional and psychological safe-house for young westerners - could in fact be disturbingly anti-intellectual and/or destructive. Of course the mainstream had long portrayed punk as the domain of nihilists, dope fiends and other assorted fuck-ups; but this was only because, in theory, the subculture was a place where even the most misanthropic shmoes could feel welcome. I saw a very real beauty in all of this. The punk scene I imagined was a place where sensitive individuals could gather to find solidarity with other disillusioned, possibly very upset people. "Sensitive" might not be the first word that comes to mind when thinking of Skinheads and punk rockers, but there's really no better description. That kind of vulnerability is often unmistakable. Yet, sensitive does not mean constructive.

As the months grew colder, hardcore punk in New Brunswick (and New Jersey in general) seemed only to heat up. Bands played all the time; so much so that often you'd have to decide *which* show you were going to attend on any particular afternoon or evening.

Up until this point, I'd put on a number of shows. But now that I had a band of my own (insert selfish motivation here), I decided to put on what I hoped would be the biggest event the Masonic Temple had ever seen. For the time, it was a killer: Boy Sets Fire, Endeavor, You and I, Staten Island's Murdock, The Degenerics and, of course, try.fail.try. With Christmas upon us, I named the show "Ho-Ho-Hardcore" and promoted it heavily. A billion kids showed up, the bands destroyed, and the show was by all measures an overwhelming success. Not to mention that it was by far the biggest and best show try.fail.try had yet played. Only one thing really sucked about that day – my band didn't have any music for people to take home.

To solve this problem, we returned to the Third Studio from the Sun early in 1998. Having had such a positive experience there recording for *Right to Assemble*, we now set our sights on a 5-song demo. And though this new recording would be put on cassette – clearly not as cool as vinyl or CD - we still wanted it to be substantial and interesting enough to really grab peoples' attention. To that end, we decided that our demo needed to come off as more than just another cassette tape. So the try.fail. try demo came in an oversized manila envelope complete with hand-screened artwork (Byrnes did most of the silk screening), as well as stickers, patches, a lyrics book and other assorted (but relevant) propaganda. We called it *Applied Ideals* and when people first saw it, the basic reaction was, "Holy crap, this is your *demo*?"

Unfortunately, none of that stuff made up for the fact that *Applied Ideals* sounded like shit. The final mix was tinny and compressed, and lacked some "mystery" property that helped make "For Freedom" seem so cool. But the songs themselves weren't bad and the tape did its job. The unique packaging and rich content got people's attention and our limited run of a few hundred tapes sold out almost immediately. With things looking up, we played every show we could and started thinking about what was next.

The cat was a kitten when he arrived at 224 unexpectedly, brought home on a whim by Annie from her job at a pet store. He was one of those tuxedo-looking cats and his name was Jabsco, after the familiar 2-Tone ska character Walt Jabsco. (You know, that famous drawing of a man in a black suit, white shirt, black tie, sunglasses, et cetera.) I suppose that none of us in the apartment had enough foresight or sense to know that 224 Hamilton Street was no place to raise a baby animal. At the very least, nobody objected at any level that could compel Annie to find a better home for the creature. He was, after all, an uncommonly robust animal, a handsome little man, and plucky enough to put up with the filth and chaos that seemed to constantly envelop 224 Hamilton Street – even if it did seem to drive him slightly crazy. Jabsco quickly became one of the crew.

Having quickly become the official house cat, it made sense for Jabsco to stay behind when Annie moved out. And since he and I had become great pals, I was more than willing to keep him in food and kitty litter. Sure, it would have been better for Jabsco to grow up somewhere else – the filth and frequent instances of extreme chaos affected this impressionable, growing creature in sad and predictable ways. But while he grew into an un-cuddly cat with a guarded personality, Jabsco was not at all timid, nor malicious. In fact, he was very social in his own way. Maybe Jabsco was something of a fuck-up, but a cat with problems isn't necessarily a *bad* cat.

Looking back, it's hard to blame Jabsco for reacting the way he did; especially considering the full-throttle insanity that often filled the air. There was yellin', and there was fightin', and in the center of it all were two constants – Tweety and alcohol.

For example: Susanna and I were laying up on my bedroom loft one night when the sound of yelling and running on the street below suddenly rushed in through my bedroom window. Figuring that it was just some standard New Brunswick jackassery, we peered out the window waiting to be entertained by whatever drunken fool happened to be getting stupid on this particular evening. But as we looked outside from the safety of my bedroom, we heard the apartment door down at ground level open and slam shut quickly. As the hurried pounding of footsteps rumbled up the stairs and into the living room, Susanna and I knew that this time we were more than spectators.

Tweety and Johnny 8-Ball bolted into the apartment. "Turn off all the lights!" yelled Tweety as he ran hurriedly to the kitchen and started drawing all the shades. They had both taken some blows to the head, but Tommy was bleeding significantly. They'd both also been maced.

Susanna and I got them some paper towels and did what we could to help. Peering guardedly through the window and trying to calm himself down, Tweety explained that he and a bunch of his friends had gotten into a huge brawl with the crowd at a party taking place in a house down the street. It was essentially Skinheads versus college kids, and it was no joke – witnesses saw dozens of people thrashing about, furniture and windows being broken, and a full-size refrigerator thrown to the floor.

With Tweety and Johnny 8-Ball quietly holed up in the darkened apartment and having done all we could, Susanna and I climbed back into the loft. As we lay silently against the windows, we watched a pickup truck full of Skinheads tear down Harvey Street, as so-called "college kids" chased them, armed with chairs, bats, and wood planks.

Spontaneous riots like this were one reason why I was spending more and more time at Susanna's dorm room over at Demarest Hall. It was quiet and relatively clean, after all – two things my apartment could never be. Sure, 224 had fulfilled its destiny of being a great punk rock headquarters, but it was a crappy and depressing place to live; not just for my new cat, but for me, too. Before long, I was avoiding the place all together.

My shitty apartment was just one more reason to be stoked when The Degenerics asked me to join them for a 10-day tour that spring. We'd be starting in Massachusetts and then heading south.

In an effort to keep the costs of the tour down, the band had decided not to rent a van from the usual car rental place. Instead, they went to a local punk dude named Rick. Rick was something of an accidental iconoclast in the Middlesex County hardcore scene; a nerdy, record-collector type with a small record distro who cut a vaguely controversial figure (at least in the New Brunswick punk universe), if not just for his general goofiness.

But renting Rick's van seemed like a good idea, so we gave him $300, packed it up, and hit the road to New England. On the way up, we saw only one problem with the vehicle, which was manageable if not unsafe and annoying. The passenger seat, it turned out, was only half-bolted into the floor of the van. This meant that every time the vehicle turned right, the person in that seat was dumped to the floor as the seat flopped sideways. Still, it was something we could laugh off, and we were saving so much money by renting Rick's van that no one would complain about such a relatively minor problem.

The tour's first show was in a basement that night in Allston - a Boston neighborhood known for music, its melting-pot environment, and, at the time, its crack heads. While the show went well enough, music wasn't what would make that night so memorable. No, that night was defined forever by what we discovered under the hood of the van as it sat parked in a convenience store parking lot. It was leaking oil; like, a lot of it. And under a closer inspection, we found that there was no cap on the oil tank. In the name of Holy Safety, we plugged it with some rags.

We were pretty pissed at Rick. It sure didn't seem like this van could handle even two days of our planned 10-day tour, yet he had rented it to us anyway. So we decided to drive the van into the ground, resigned to conjuring up a way home if and when we got stranded. The next show on the tour was the following day in Baltimore, coincidentally with Worthless. It was getting late, and we were pissed and determined. I volunteered to drive, everyone piled in, and we began heading south.

It was probably around 3 a.m. when I started to feel like I was falling asleep at the wheel. And while I was definitely tired, there was no reason for me to feel like I was going to pass out. Wondering if anyone else would be willing to take drive, I first turned to the passenger seat, where Frank was sitting, nodding off. Then I looked into the back of the van, wondering if anyone else might be awake, when I realized that the entire back of the van was enveloped in a cloud. It was only then that I noticed the steady flow of smoke pouring through the dashboard, into the van's interior. I wasn't tired or stoned – I was being gassed.

Alarmed to say the least, I pulled the van over abruptly and in a loud and panicky voice ordered everyone out. We emptied ourselves onto the desolate highway, bleary-eyed and, for the most part, confused. Pat, for example, stood there in his boxer shorts, squinting and clutching a box of Honeycomb cereal. There in the dark Connecticut hills, we opened the hood to see that burning oil had spattered all over the place, covering the guts of the car. The resulting smoke was heading straight into the van through the dash, slowly poisoning us.

Realizing that we needed a new plan, we continued south, our anger percolating. By morning we somehow managed to get that heap of shit back to New Brunswick. Not sure of how to move forward, we stopped at the Edison Diner for some food, rest, and planning. First, we'd go and get our money back from Rick; then we'd hit Fleming's house and regroup.

In our haste, we neglected to call Rick to warn him that we'd be stopping by with a score to settle – and he was pretty surprised when we rang his doorbell early that morning. Perhaps the unexpectedness and early hour were why Rick initially resisted giving us a refund. Nonetheless, we were very convincing. He had, after all, ruined the tour and all the work that went into it by renting us a steaming hot turd of a vehicle.

Fleming was the second guy surprised to see us at his front door that morning. After all, he sent us off with well wishes not 24 hours prior. Ever sympathetic and solid, he let us hang out and use his phone to call the dudes in Worthless. We arranged for a ride and some equipment sharing for that night's show in Baltimore. At least The Degenerics would get to play two of the shows planned for their tour instead of one. The Worthless caravan soon arrived to pick us up, and both bands and their associated rogues headed south. Someone gave me a hot foot while I was asleep in the van, which I didn't think was funny.

By April of 1998, try.fail.try had become active enough to worry Pat. Concerned that the band was distracting P-Nut from The Degenerics (and that Fanshen was having an equally hampering effect on his and Frank's time), Pat declared that the "side bands" would have to cool off. Admittedly, it was a time in which inflated expectations of The Degenerics had a number of people (including myself) imagining big things for the future. Pat saw Fanshen and try.fail.try as somehow standing between the band and its intended destiny. And while The Degenerics was always P-Nut's priority, he didn't seem to share Pat's level of concern (which ultimately faded anyway), so we continued to do our thing. And as it should have been, each time we played it felt better and more natural. We were tightening our songs, refining our sound, and getting to play with bands we loved, from Ink and Dagger to The Dillinger Escape Plan to Kid Dynamite. It was almost like we were a real band.

Spending so much of my time and creative steam on try.fail. try had, however, continued to impact *Aneurysm* in a negative way, and half way though the production of issue #11 I decided to stop publishing the zine all together. At first it was difficult to abandon my trusted ambassador. I had poured my heart (and money) into *Aneurysm* for over four years, and it had come fairly far. But I knew the reality – that my media obsession, which sat at the core of *Aneurysm,* needed to grow, and that try.fail.try offered it the opportunity to do so.

Change seemed to be the order of the day anyhow.

Nobody wanted to live in the Chateau Ghetto any more. (Go figure that the novelty of living in a squalid punk flophouse would wear off.) While we weren't necessarily sick of each other, Tweety, Crawford, Frank and I nonetheless agreed to go our separate ways. (In turn, no one gave a shit about the cokehead ringer our landlord had found to replace Annie when she moved out.) Crawford would return to his parents' house after graduation, and Tweety planned to move in with his girlfriend and Little Pedro. And though Frank was one of my closest friends, he'd been through a rough patch and hadn't been the most reliable room mate. So as try.fail.try played a basement show on Plum Street that May, I conspired with four other kids to start the next chapter of my punk rock situation.

At the end of May came the unthinkable – graduation. Originally, I hadn't planned to participate in the Rutgers commencement activities (as I imagined myself to be in staunch ideological opposition to all ceremonies and rituals), but friends and family had convinced me to rock the cap and gown anyway. In the end, I was glad that I went; not because of the pomp and circumstance (which I really still hated), but because it seemed to make my folks and Susanna happy. Plus had I not gone to graduation, I wouldn't have seen Fleming streaking across Voorhees Mall (the big collegiate Rutgers lawn in the center of campus) in my honor.

Still, I was underwhelmed. For a college graduate, I felt remarkably ill-prepared for life in the real world. I was also disgusted by the prospect of employment, mostly because I saw careerism as a dangerous perversion of the human experience. Still, I'd have to pay my bills and spend my time doing something other than writing acerbic term papers about the decline of western culture. So I got a job at the New Brunswick Kinko's and it wasn't necessarily awesome. But I had my girl, my band, and my friends – and that was pretty good to me.

Six – 1998-2000: 20 Huntington

During my year as a refugee from filth/resident of 224 Hamilton Street, I spent lots of time visiting friends. And of all the New Brunswick apartments and houses I spent time in, 20 Huntington Street had always been my favorite. Adolfo and Casey had lived there with some other dudes and each time I visited them I couldn't help but sweat their digs. In comparison to 224 Hamilton Street, 20 Huntington Street was palatial.

The house sat on one of the more picturesque blocks near the College Avenue Campus and had many qualities that made it comfortable and just plain nice - a large, gated back yard; front and back porches (great for bikes, chillin', or sleeping); a three-car driveway, and a great kitchen with modern cabinets and appliances. All the rooms were clean and in good condition, and with its dark hardwood floors, wide stair case, and general spaciousness, 20 Huntington was rich, warm, and inviting – aesthetics that had been sorely lacking in my life.

But moving into 20 Huntington wasn't only about a change of scenery. The dynamic between me and my new roommates was, after all, completely different than what I'd experienced over the last few years. Byrnes – now my band mate *and* my roommate - was extremely clean and way into physical fitness. Red-head Sue had long given up shop-lifting and played guitar all of the time, in both Stormshadow with Crawford, as well as with a short-lived but great Jawbreaker-esque band called Rock,Star that Zak had started. Sue had lots of records and was always up on the latest band sure to change the world. And Casey and Tom were reserved and vaguely introverted, but in different ways. I already knew both of them for a few years and anticipated that they'd be mild-mannered roommates – they were, after all, two very low-key dudes. And while they did pop open in startling ways when performing with their band You and I, both Tom and Casey both stayed quietly in their rooms most of the time.

This was a totally different type of "punk house" than what I was used to, but it was a good fit. Instead of drunken, directionless hysteria, this new collection of rogues had an almost bookish quality. Everyone was vegetarian or vegan, and except for me everyone was straight-edge. No more drunken Skinheads brawling in the street. No more holes in the walls. No more forbidden rooms and no more filth. I was psyched to say the least.

I took the attic, which was huge and finished, complete with wall-to-wall carpet and a private stair case leading up from behind a door on the second floor. A wall built by Adolfo (the room's previous inhabitant) divided the space into two separate parts. I turned the back area into my bedroom, and the large front portion into my office-slash-den of iniquity. Since no one was legally allowed to live up there, we told the landlord that I lived at my girlfriend's apartment (which was partially true), and that the attic space was being rented as an office and lounge for when I was "working." Throughout the coming year the landlord would occasionally interrogate us as to why there was a mattress on the floor, or a dresser full of clothes - but we kept up the story, and he couldn't prove that it wasn't true. And he *did* cash our rent checks.

I was also glad to be providing a better environment for Jabsco. Since being promoted from accidental pal to my full-time pet, he'd grown into a large, lean, and muscular beast – in many ways, he was the Kareem Abdul Jabar of cats. It had always made me sad that the apartment at 224 Hamilton was so cat-unfriendly, so moving to a gigantic house with three floors and no crazy motherfuckers trying to grab his tail was definitely a step up; even if Jabsco would have to deal with Chloe, Byrnes' sketchy runt of a feline. She was small, ran kind of crooked, and her lower lip was all mashed up - not to mention that the cat was completely crazy. For example, Chloe would sweetly hop up on your lap for affection, and then claw your face once she had enough. This sort of behavior didn't make her terribly popular with people, or with Jabsco. Luckily, the house was big enough for the two of them to easily avoid one another.

And yet with so many reasons to be psyched about 20 Huntington Street, the filthy basement was the building's most important feature. True, it was loaded with old books and magazines, busted shelving, broken furniture, and all sorts of other useless crap - but Byrnes, Sue, Tom and I were determined to make it into a punk rock basement, suitable for shows and band practices. With permission from the landlord, the overwhelming clutter was cleared in one very long day of hard work, revealing a space more than adequate for what we had in mind. To me, all of this was a huge deal – I had always wanted to live in a space where shows could happen.

The shows came almost immediately. We started small and usually included at least one of the house bands each time. By the time You and I did the record release show for *Within the Frame* down there that August, we'd ironed all of the kinks out of our ghetto PA system and kids were showing up on a regular basis. We didn't imagine that our basement would be a substitute for the Melody Bar or anything like that, but we were able to offer a reliable and regular place for bands to play - and that was great.

Toward the end of the summer it became clear that my job at Kinko's wasn't paying enough. Sure, it was a jackpot for the hardcore kid in me. After all, the Kinko's corporation had been a very helpful corporate partner to the hardcore punk community of the 90s, and working there allowed me to carry on the rich tradition of punk rockers working at Kinko's and stealing *everything*. But as far as jobs go, mine sucked; and it felt lousy to not have any money or a plan. Sensing that my destiny didn't lie in the world of retail document reproduction, I sent my resume to a couple of comic book companies that never replied, and interviewed at a creepy public relations company in Manhattan. They offered me a job I couldn't imagine taking. Nothing was happening.

Susanna and I started to have problems and as the leaves fell, so did we - into an awful slump. Admirably, we discussed our problems and optimistically vowed to make things work. But in reality, our relationship was ending. We still spent time together – but it was pointless hanging-on, mostly on my part I suspect.

Red-head Sue got me an interview at the place where she was working at the time. The job involved doing tech support for an email server on campus. And although I was skeptical – certainly, I was not a systems administrator – I went on the interview anyway. Now I was pretty good with computers and I told them that. But I had no experience running a Unix-based email system, and I told them that too. Still, I said that I was a fast learner, and that with the proper training I'd probably be fine. They hired me, and after the first week I knew conclusively that, for a number of reasons, this was not the job for me. But the money was okay, and I really needed it.

Doing work I didn't care about just for the cash – well, it insulted every notion I had of myself as a young neo-Marxist. It was nauseating. But in retrospect, this was all a timely and nicely sobering slap of material reality. After all, I'd now spent years theorizing and mentally deconstructing everything in society so that I could offer my oh-so-insightful criticisms. In truth, I'd remained happily trapped in my head until push really started coming to shove with the real world. More than ever, daily life now demanded that I reconcile my ideals with my material needs and move along, thank you. It was a forced collision of theory and practice, and in an over-arching way it darkened my mood. Figure in my floundering relationship with Susanna and the fact that I'd never been so fat in my entire life, and it left a constant taste of dog shit in my mouth. I hated myself.

You know that notion that struggle and misery are good for art? Well, if anything in my own personal experience ever confirmed that theory, then this period of my life was it, because try.fail.try was in full fucking effect. We played all the time, some kids knew the words, and once in a while I'd even see someone wearing one of our t-shirts. We were like, a *band* now. So when Vasilios Daskalopoulos offered to put out our first proper record – well, it made perfect sense.

Vasil had long been a fixture of the central Jersey hardcore scene. He was immediately identifiable as one of those cool and brilliant people who make life extra interesting; a real one-of-a-kind guy. Years before, he had a small skate clothing company called 9Volt. Now resurrected as 9Volt Discs, Vasil had taken on a partner in one very tall Brian B. and started putting out records. (Although it never achieved much growth or commercial success, 9Volt Discs would ultimately document a significant chunk of the hardcore and punk coming out of New Jersey in the mid-to-late 90s, putting out some classic records in the process – the first God Forbid record, the Strength 691 discography, and essential releases from For The Love Of…, The Degenerics, Worthless, Stormshadow, Fanshen and others.)

Intent on a really good recording, we convinced Vasil to

send us to the well-known New Jersey studio Trax East, where we spent three very hectic days with producer Steve Evetts. It was an awesome experience. Not only were we recording in an amazing studio on someone else's dime, but we were working with the guy who'd recorded Deadguy's *Fixation on a Coworker*, *Progression Through Unlearning* by Snapcase, and Hatebreed's genre-defining classic, *Satisfaction Is the Death of Desire*. And though none of us could have imagined how Steve's resume would continue to grow over the coming years, we still knew that the record we were making had the potential to be pretty fucking cool. And hey, who knew Adolfo was playing an entire song out of key? Thanks, Steve!

Despite the abundant awesomeness, there was one rub: the final day of our recording was also the day of Endeavor's last show. It was a conflict we'd known about for a while, but we were bummed now that it was actually taking place. All of us in try.fail.try were Endeavor fans, and through hardcore, hanging out and New Brunswick we'd all become good friends. So yeah, it sucked to miss their final performance. But we couldn't have had a better excuse. Instead of focusing on something that was ending, we were helping to create something new. We remained determined to do our best, even it meant missing Endeavor's last show.

Ironically, Endeavor vocalist Mike O. joined try.fail.try as a second guitarist a few weeks later. He'd been a fan of the band since we started, and having him join made perfect sense to all of us. Additionally, we now had two gigantic guitar-playing bodybuilders, which was pretty funny. And given the way everything outside of my band was going, I was glad to have something – anything – to laugh at.

Winter crept closer and Casey moved out. He was replaced by Daniel Wharton, a teenage computer genius who loved positive hardcore and making soup in his crock pot. Dan was also friends with John Waverka, Sue's unofficial live-in boyfriend and the singer for a hardcore band called The Purpose. (Other members eventually wound up in Thursday, Saves The Day, and a number of other Jersey bands.) Both Daniel and John would eventually become my close friends, but at this time they were little more to me than two younger, very weird dudes. That's not to say that either of them was unpleasant – quite the contrary. In different ways, both John and Dan really added to the distinct spirit that ran throughout the house at 20 Huntington Street. And I needed all the spirit I could get.

I spent Christmas in Rhode Island, trying to squeeze the last few drops of enjoyment from my relationship with Susanna. Not wanting to stay through the New Year (and consciously deciding not to be with my girlfriend on New Year's Eve), I took a miserable train ride back to New Brunswick the day after Christmas. No one was around to pick me up from the train station, and after walking a mile through the cold night back to 20 Huntington Street with my large duffel bag, I arrived to a deserted, pitch black house. Everyone I knew was somewhere else, my first love and I were in shambles, and my job – well, it was just some job. Here I stood facing a big empty house with nothing to do once I went inside. I didn't even want to open the door.

But it was cold outside, so I turned my key and pushed the knob into the darkness of the house. In the living room on the left, two small sets of glimmering eyes peered from the couch. "How cute," I thought. Jabsco and Chloe were finally hanging out. At least *something* positive was going on.

But when I turned on the light, I didn't see Jabsco and Chloe cuddling up on the couch. Instead, I found myself looking perplexedly at two kittens I'd never seen before. One was a rusty black, and the other was a stripey, yellow pear-shaped number with no tail. They just kind of sat there and stared at me. Hey, what could have been better than kittens for a glum chum like me, right? I soon learned that Byrnes had gotten them as a Christmas gift for his dad, who wound up not wanting them. The one with no tail liked to make burpy purring noises and her name became Bailey. The black Burmese was possibly the friendliest cat ever, and Byrnes called him Turbo. And since the house at 20 Huntington was so expansive, with so many areas and nooks and crannies to explore, it would have been a crime *not* to have four cats living there.

But despite kittens and general attempts to "stay posi," I was definitely having a rough time. New Years' Eve was lonely, New Brunswick was empty for me, and I was way bummed. 1999. End of the world, ma.

Under most circumstances, I would have been thankful for anything that could snap me out of such a depressing funk. But when it came to the catalyst for change this time around – well I would have gladly stayed depressed if it meant undoing such grim inspiration. My friend Matt Leveton had been badly injured in a car accident.

I first met Matt at one of the many shows he put on at the Manville Elks Lodge. Together with another kid named Benny Horowitz, he helped to establish that place as a major axle of the New Jersey punk and hardcore scene of the 1990s. Over the years, I'd grown to know Matt quite well, and we always enjoyed seeing one another. And though he'd recently moved to South Carolina, Matt's Jersey roots ran deep; I had even slept on his floor a few times in recent months as The Degenerics repeatedly rolled through Columbia.

So Matt's accident was unsettling to say the least, not to mention that only months earlier an eerily similar tragedy had befallen Adam D., a former classmate of mine and bass player for local metal heads the Dillinger Escape Plan. So like they'd done for Adam and so many others before, the proverbial kids channeled their shock and heartache into a reaction that could have real-world results.

Matt didn't have medical insurance, but for years he paid into a system of kids, bands, music and ideas – sometimes with his wallet, but mostly with his heart and spirit. So in returning the favor, bands and kids came out in droves to demonstrate their support. The first (and arguably most memorable) benefit show was a now-legendary two-day event at, of course, the Manville Elks lodge. It included Sick of It All, Ensign, Kid Dynamite, Kill Your Idols, Stretch Armstrong, The Low End Theory, Nora, Clubber Lang, Where Fear and Weapons Meet, and a special and much-hyped reunion of Strength 691. Day two saw performances from Agnostic Front, Vision, For the Love Of..., Indecision, The Degenerics, Purpose, Reach the Sky, Skycamefalling, Step Ahead and Stormshadow. Benny (with help from Ensign vocalist Tim Shaw) did a truly amazing job booking and promoting the weekend, and as expected both days were completely off the hook. Matt's mom made an inspiring speech, Morris County Youth Crew legend (and New Brunswick ultra-scenester) Paul Hanly got his nose smashed into a bloody mess during Vision's set, and most importantly (at least in the immediate sense), thousands of dollars were raised. In the long run, of course, the money was a drop in Matt's bucket. But then again, the show was about much more than just money.

There were a few more benefit shows to follow and thanks to Chris Ross try.fail.try was able to play a couple of them. In New York, we rocked with The Movielife, Ensign, Kill Your

Idols, Nora, Skycamefalling, Two Man Advantage and a band called Daybreak. About a month later we were honored with yet another chance to mosh for Matt, this time at the Melody Bar in good old New Brunswick with Stretch Armstrong, Good Clean Fun, Torn Apart, Zao, Buried Alive, Atom & His Package, You and I, and Murdock.

By now I'd been involved with numerous benefit shows. I even briefly held the opinion that *all* shows should be benefit shows - admittedly extreme, but not when you feel like the world is in a constant state of crisis, bursting with need. For a long time I'd seen a natural connection between fund raising and punk rock; it kept a nice, tidy civic element in play, lest the kids forget that their problems are connected to a bigger world. But these shows for Matt were different from all of that. Here was someone I knew well, suddenly paralyzed for life, and in reaction I was sent reeling. It brought everything so much closer. This wasn't about saving an arts collective or freeing a political prisoner I'd never met. It was about helping a friend. A friend I knew *only* because of music.

In retrospect, this whole set of events underscores an interesting distinction between the kinds of benefit shows. On the one hand, there are the ones intended to raise money for a social or political cause or organization. On the other hand, there are shows intended to raise money for an individual (or family) who has met some unfortunate circumstance, usually related to health or physical well-being. And while, theoretically, benefits for organizations or political causes are about the well-being of *all* people, folks are generally more passionate about helping a fallen friend than they are in funding grass-roots organizations. Some might say that's a small-minded tendency, revealing how selfish we can be in our acts of charity - that we rally to those we know and ignore those we don't. Nonetheless I wanted to play for Matt more intensely than I'd ever wanted to play for any reason in my life, because he was my friend, and because his love for hardcore punk and life had always been an inspiration to me. It was a privilege and an honor. To me, *this* was hardcore.

Meanwhile, over at my email job, I was fired for incompetence. My bosses told me it was because I failed to properly administer the email system. When I reminded the bosses that I'd come into the job clearly declaring that I didn't have the right skills, they just kind of blinked and said nothing. It didn't bother me – I was glad to never sit in that stale cubicle ever again.

I strode out of that boring place for the last time feeling energized and free - if not just for that moment - and later on that same warm winter day I started the process to become a substitute teacher. Mike O. had been doing it for a while and said it was a good gig, and at least a school environment wouldn't be completely foreign. In the couple of months it took for everything to be finalized, I collected unemployment and did a whole lot of hanging out, especially with food and the internet. With way too much time to think, I sort of let myself turn into a sad sack. Any self-destructive tendencies I had reached their sordid peak, and I started to find my own lack of inspiration to be depressing at best.

The try.fail.try seven inch was released – at least *that* was good. It was on white wax and had a color cover, and as a band we were pretty psyched on how the songs had come out. *We Deal In Lives* revealed real growth for us, and on a personal level I was ecstatic to have a seven inch record of my very own. It was another thing so many of my friends and all of my bandmates had already experienced – but not me. Not until now. Still, this singular high point had little impact on the inertia of my day to day life.

After a few months of said nothingness, my paperwork cleared and I began working as a sub. And though the money was shitty, the work itself was good; especially in the cushy schools of neighboring Highland Park. Plus, I was lucky enough to get a cool assignment early on - a long-term gig filling in for a high school Social Studies teacher who developed pneumonia. This meant that over those few weeks I actually had to be a teacher to these kids, as opposed to just showing up for a day and handing out worksheets. And it went really well; so well, in fact, that I was sent spinning. I hadn't expected to find so much satisfaction from interacting with those students. But the truth was that it rivaled the rush I'd experienced with *Aneurysm* and then try.fail. try. And strangely, my media obsession roared. Was it really a *communication* obsession? After all, I'd made plenty of speeches between songs at try.fail.try shows. Was that really so different than explaining to high school kids how corporate lobbyists control Congress?

For all of the excitement, the idea of teaching was nonetheless a bitter pill at first; primarily because I had so many conceptual and ideological problems with formalized education. By the time I'd finished my sentence in American public schools, I really, really resented them. So how could a revolutionary hardcore punk rocker possibly justify working within a system so clearly fraught with bullshit – or for the state, no less? Not to mention the concept of having a job that requires one to wake up so unbelievably early. Theoretically, it was a losing proposition. But something unexpected came from the few short weeks I spent with the kids at Highland Park High School: I liked teaching, and teaching was work. Therefore, I liked work.

This was a powerful realization. Forced by the world to reconcile my material needs with my idealism, I'd come up empty for almost a year. But now I found something that could both put food on my table *and* allow me to fight the good fight (as I saw it). And not only that; the actual work of the job kept me interested, and spoke to things I cared about. My whole life, I'd felt as if most people in the world didn't have a lick of passion in their lives. In so many ways, *Aneurysm* and try.fail. try helped me to reach out and encourage people to care about life - because we're here, and we might as well do our best. I wanted to scream, "You can do something awesome!", or "You can get through your struggles!" And sure, our old friend the Dominant Power Structure has always been a huge part of how we think about learning and teaching. But even within those 50-minute blocks, it felt like I could really make a difference. Not to mention the urgency of the job, in the most immediate sense. It's rarely possible for a teacher to sleep on the job. (Though I have seen it done.)

So yeah, substitute teaching. It made me want to wake up early every day. Go figure.

As far as my ideas on schools and learning - or life, for that matter – well, I didn't know shit; a fact that was repeatedly highlighted for me time and time again over the next few years. The importance of the moment was simply that I'd found a work environment in which I felt comfortable, and interested, and willing to try. All in all, it was a somewhat dramatic turn of events for a guy who weeks prior had no idea of what to do with life and hated the notion of employment. I subbed as much as possible, and took it seriously every time. And almost every time, it was good.

In March I found myself back in New Bedford, Massachusetts. Despite the many hours of travel I'd now logged thanks to punk rock, I somehow hadn't managed to get back there since tagging along with Lifetime three years prior. But this time I had a much better reason to be there – to rock the motherfucking house at New Bedford Fest 1999.

Nora and try.fail.try rolled up to the show together and played. A lot of other bands played, too – housemates-slash-sensitive dudes You and I and metalcore pioneers For The Love Of... helped represent for Jersey, alongside bands like Ink and Dagger, Grade, Piebald, and 400 Years. And while a fun time was surely had by all, my most vivid memory of that particular weekend was Mike O. and his amazing blazing ass. The wacky muscle-man shakes he drank all the time were not only causing unbelievable smells to constantly pour out of him. They were straining relations with multiple friends, band mates, and roadies. The dude's ass was a toxic dump.

As the months got warmer, try.fail.try continued to venture out of New Jersey, but probably not as much as we should have. We played a couple shows in Virginia – Richmond and Blacksburg – and hit up Philly once or twice. But The Degenerics were always P-Nut's priority, and that was limiting. Still, our record was out and things were going pretty well, so we did as much as we could; and most of the time that meant playing shows relatively close to home. And while it probably would have been cool for us to play more out-of-state shows, there were worse places to be stuck than Jersey.

If I couldn't travel extensively and plant seeds along the way, at least I could help tend a garden at home. The basement at 20 Huntington Street was becoming a reliable guerilla venue, featuring not only the house bands and the bands we ourselves met out on the road, but touring bands placing cold calls, wanting to play our basement on their way through town. Soon enough they were coming from all over the place; California, Virginia, New England, Chicago, and Staten Island - and they almost always had a great time.

Is it hopeful and naive to say that most of the kids who played our basement weren't hoping to become rock stars? Sure, Green Day and The Offspring and Blink 182 had demonstrated that the pop side of punk rock could be brought to the masses. But most of the music many of us loved seemed too aggressive to be commercially viable on any large scale. So many of the bands that came to 20 Huntington Street were downright explosive – maybe even intimidating to someone who never experienced that intense, personal kind of music played in one of the most intimate settings possible.

It was heavenly to me. Through what was arguably just a new prescription for my punk rock rose colored glasses, I saw a party (pun intended) concerned with expression, community, and honesty of mind and heart. There could be a rich, complex and emotional relationship with music – especially when it was performed live in a setting like the basement at 20 Huntington Street – and that is what my friends and I had. We were the ones who played like our lives depended on it. We screamed lyrics into microphones and meant every single syllable as much as we could. We took turns cracking our chests open and spilling our guts – using music and anti-ritual to cleanse and learn. Melodies and words reflected our real fears, real sadness, real anger, and real dreams. And most of us could smell a bullshit band a mile away. 20 Huntington Street was not a place for bullshit rock and roll. This was not Sugar Ray. This was fucking Devoid of Faith. Saetia. The Cable Car Theory. Dead Nation. Kill The Man Who Questions. Majority Rule. The Exploder. And while everyone had to know that it wouldn't last forever, the meantime was incredibly fulfilling.

As much of an eye-opener as substitute teaching had been, the work was sporadic and didn't pay well. And although I was starting to sense that I could actually do something with my life *and* enjoy it, I still needed to make more money. Luckily the girl I was now dating - who'd gone to Rutgers and, coincidentally, also to my high school - helped me out. She didn't just find me a job – she found me an opportunity that would change my life forever.

Through a mixture of fear and ignorance, lots of folks – especially kids - have an aversion to people with profound disabilities. Whether it's the retarded kid down the street or the adult with Downs Syndrome who works at the local WalMart, most "regular folk" don't exactly offer a friendly embrace when it comes to the disabled. Even those with purely physical disabilities due to illness or accident usually often get dissed by the greater society. I like Howard Stern, but that's some straight-up exploitation when he uses disabled people as punch lines. I like my friend Billy (fabricated for this example), but I still think he's an asshole for parking in a handicapped spot so he can "save some time." What's our problem? Do we see something in their disability that we fear or don't like about ourselves? Or are "they" so different from us that we just can't handle it? Whatever the reason, most people like to pretend that profound disability doesn't exist. It's simply too disturbing to our little pea-brains.

At least, it was to *my* little pea brain.

So when I arrived on that warm spring day to meet Dr. Gerhardt and try to get a job as a teaching assistant, I was skeptical. After all, The Douglass Developmental Disabilities Center exclusively served people with varying shades of autism. And while these individuals often start specialized treatment as early as age three, the job I was trying to get was with the Adult & Transition Services division. This stand-alone division had only eight students (or "clients" depending on their age), but many of them were just as big if not bigger than me. And this program was geared toward individuals with profound developmental disability; too often, that meant extreme behavior problems including aggression, destruction of objects, doors, or walls, and other wacky kinds of outbursts. At least half of me didn't know what I was doing there at all.

But Dr. Gerhardt offered me the job with dizzying speed - and since I *had* gone there to, you know, *get* said job, I immediately accepted. At which point I was asked if I clearly understood that I'd be getting hurt at work. I nodded in the affirmative, but in reality I didn't think I'd last a week.

But I did – and suddenly found myself waking up early every morning and going to, uh... work? Most of the students/clients I was working with had problems with things like speech and hygiene, so a big part of the job was to work toward maximizing quality of life. The clinical approach used for this daunting task was called Applied Behavior Analysis, or ABA – and this method was used to drill such basics as counting money and sorting items by type. Sure, there were academic lessons like reading and math, but we also spent time teaching Johnny not to stick his fingers in his butt and then lick them. And all of this, of course, required close physical contact with the students.

While my first on-the-job injury was pretty damn startling (a quick and unexpected head butt which sent me to the hospital), I quickly got used to the situation. Soon enough I'd be racking up broken noses and concussions like nobody's business. My hands often looked as if I'd been wrestling with weasels – bite marks and little slices merging into one mashed-up, sore, throbbing wound. One particularly large chap pitched me down a flight of stairs. Another guy smacked the hell out of my jaw, just because I wanted to help him make his lunch.

Of course, the physicality of the job quickly became one trivial aspect of a much larger picture. Inside of me, something was waking up – and as I learned the nuances of each student's personality, I broke a little further past my own preconceptions and fears about folks with these kinds of problems. I reflected on how huge a jackass I'd been without even knowing it until now. Maybe I should have caught on earlier; then again, out of sight out of mind, you know? But the experience re-made me, like the time I sat on the red rug and listened to Operation Ivy. And while it's safe to say that change is happening all the time, there was nothing gradual about my trial by fire in the field of special education. Lucky for me, in this case the process of enlightenment was expeditious and arresting.

I thought about all of my hardcore punk rocker friends. I thought about how forward-thinking I considered myself, yet how unaware I'd been – unaware regarding disabilities, and unaware regarding my own prejudices and subjectivity. I thought about people laughing at "retards" on television or in public. I thought about my friends with mental health issues like OCD and depression, and wondered if I ever treated them poorly without knowing it. I thought about the urgent call for social justice and realized that, like me, so much of what came from punk rock had been limited, and limiting. How we treat each other – through governments, schools, religions, et cetera – is, after all, what punk and hardcore are all about. Not that I'm attempting a definition here – just that, whatever this thing is, it's somehow connected to the social evolution of humanity. Some of the activists I knew used to say things like, "We speak for those who cannot speak for themselves." A lot of times they meant animals, or forests, or prisoners, or poor people. Here I was, faced with that same notion, but in a dramatically different iteration than any cause commonly championed by the kids or the scene. Media obsession or communication obsession or whatever else be damned – I shot toward the experience like an arrow.

It was transformative; and though the pay was once again amazingly awful, this job soon seemed like the most meaningful thing I had ever done on a day-to-day basis. To me, it was more punk rock than punk rock: the privilege of teaching and advocating for a population forever marginalized by so-called "normal" human beings. Historically, people with profound disabilities have suffered shockingly inhuman treatment; and it's not like the world's most intensive and sophisticated program has any hope of "fixing" a person with profound autism, retardation, or OCD. But that's where you have to question destination versus journey, or progress versus process. This is crucial: the way in which civil society deals with the fringes of its population is directly related to how members of that society deal with their closest friends and associates, face to face. Read that again if you need to. Wouldn't most people enjoy a more loving, peaceful, and fair world? This now meant that I had to look at myself – that if I wanted to be an agent of change or peace, I'd have to commit to a constant struggle against my own fears and unintentional misdeeds. I'd have to commit to drawing people in, instead of pushing them away, the way the world wanted me to.

"Punk is what you make of it." So I took some things I'd learned from punk rock and otherwise, and tried something new. After all, isn't innovation always at the center of the greatest, most impacting ideas and moments? In the long run, aren't specific costumes, spectacles, and songs incidental among the rushing, crushing current of the human story? Yes, there's that sweet spot - where you can make something about life better while we're all here together. And in that spirit, I'd spent years worrying about people using money and guns to kill each other over land, profit, or prophets, while cures and solutions waited undiscovered. But now I had a chance to connect my daily experience to the discovery of solutions, and to do it on a most personal level. In the fight for social justice, I found my most meaningful front-line position yet.

I gained confidence I barely knew was missing. I learned about myself and gained new perspective on what it meant to be a person, dealing with people – whether disabled or "normal." Not to mention that I'd learned a little physical pain wasn't the end of the world, especially if going through it meant helping someone to have a better life. I may have gotten the shit kicked out of me here and there, but the bigger picture was... bigger.

Summer arrived, with Tommy and Byrnes both moving out of 20 Huntington Street. Needing to save money, Byrnes went to his mom's house in nearby Middlesex. Tommy, on the other hand, was just done with it. And by "it," I pretty much mean me and Byrnes.

Anyone who knew the two of us in those days knew where our heads were when it came to issues of race, gender, homophobia, et cetera – after all, try.fail.try was by this point established as an outspoken "political" band and the aforementioned (arguably oversimplified) issues were the very foundation of the type of hardcore we aimed to play. As a band and as individuals, we sure as hell weren't aligned with the capitalist, racist, sexist, homophobic establishment. Or at least we tried not to be.

Still, we were human beings, so for whatever reason our sense of humor behind closed doors was especially extreme - perhaps even epic. Maybe Tom didn't appreciate our nearly theatrical sarcasm, because he seemed to believe that both Chris Byrnes and I were homophobic, racist hate mongers. Of course we found this reaction to be completely hilarious and unexpected, and it offered an irresistible invitation to irony we'd never even considered possible. Maybe Tommy just didn't accept the idea of making a dodgy joke for the sake of satire; that because bigotry is absurd in the first place, there's a good chuckle to be had by imitating bigots. Never bothering to ask me and Byrnes outright to explain ourselves, Tommy soon split out of the house. Perhaps dick and fart jokes just weren't his thing.

A 19-year old girl named Corry took Tommy's room. She was young and pretty, and had been hanging around the New Brunswick punk and hardcore scene for a while. Corry was friends with Sue, but I already knew her from her association with a fairly visible animal rights group that often intersected with hardcore punk in New Jersey. She was one of those vaguely crunchy militant vegan hardcore activist types. Once, I even arrived home to find two FBI agents questioning her. Fun.

Byrnes was replaced by a kid named Clay, who previously lived at 331 Somerset Street and had done a bunch of shows there. I'd seen lots of bands at 331, from Death Threat to Kill Your Idols to Hot Water Music to Kid Dynamite. try.fail.try had played there too, so through all of this I'd gotten to know Clay quite well, as well as his roommate Geoff. I first met Geoff about a year prior in the Rutgers computer lab; he said he was a fan of try.fail.try, we chatted, and he gave me a copy of his band's demo. While it had some rough edges for sure, the music seemed sincere. Since I also knew their guitar player Tom from his last band, and since Geoff was so nice, it was easy to like Thursday - even if they were still finding their voice.

Summer flew by and although the money was still tight, I felt remarkably refreshed and rebooted. I stopped eating chocolate pudding and started working out, dropping 25 pounds and going from flab to fab in only three months. And while things went south with the girl who'd gotten me my job (she still worked downstairs – comfortable!), I was nonetheless stoked to be single. I was – how you say? – ready to mingle.

Despite the functional mediocrity of my financial outlook, I was quite content. I'd grown accustomed to leaning on my front porch with friends, and spending time on things that felt vital and rewarding. I had a cat. I'd recovered from a rough patch in my love life, ditched the negativity, and spent a lot of time at the Melody Bar having a good time – not only on Sunday afternoons, but on Tuesday nights, too. My friends and I were the best fucking thing on planet Earth, and I had another punk rock summer in New Brunswick.

With autumn on the horizon I booked a Sunday matinee for the basement. The bill was good - Nora, Fast Times, Garrison and of course, try.fail.try – and I was intent on making it an involving, awesome event. But despite how at peace I felt with the universe, I wasn't infallible. I would get my involving, awesome event – plus a whole lot of other junk.

Now by this point, I'd grown to consider Carl from Nora a friend. Though we weren't necessarily calling each other to hang out on Friday nights, the two of us had grown to know one another well through the years, and had always gotten along. Carl had advertised for Ferret in *Aneurysm*, we traveled and played shows together, and once he even raised the possibility of putting out a try.fail.try record. So the big picture looked a lot like friendship to me.

This was why I was so surprised when, one day before the show, Fleming presented me with a printout from the "rants" section of the Ferret Music website. It was an angry, judgmental diatribe about 30 or so "dirty" and "PC" kids from New Brunswick that represented a separate clique than his within our common little corner of Jersey. Carl's rant questioned everything about these kids, and it was aggressive. If memory serves, it included the phrase "don't know shit about shit."

What else was I supposed to think? There was, after all, some space between our respective crews, even though we intermingled regularly and even shared scattered band members. And yes, the ambiguous "we" did our thing, and the equally ambiguous "they" did their thing. But none of that implied any kind of animosity, at least on my part. Still, Carl's rant clearly seemed to be about me and my friends. It was troubling – and beyond the general duplicity, I was about to host the guy's band in my basement. Suddenly, Carl was a no-good two-faced motherfucker - and I was pissed.

I showed the print-out to everyone I could, and then posted it in the kitchen. I pointed it out to every guest that came through in the hours before the show, and a number of people got really angry, really quickly. The bands arrived, the kids showed up, and it was on.

Fast Times and Garrison played. Then came try.fail.try. Between songs, I made a comment about $50 underwear, directed at Carl and his designer boxer briefs. It was a cheap dig, and I didn't care – this was my house, and at least half of the room was with me. We finished our set and broke down our gear, tension in the air. Nora was next.

It was Fid who brought the fire. Sure, most of the people in our little crew thought Carl was talking about us and that he was a dick for doing so. But as Nora played, Fid carried the printout down to the basement and shoved it in Carl's face, demanding an explanation. It was uncomfortable, and confrontational, and not constructive; still, we thought we were right. For the most part, I think that Carl and the guys in Nora were caught off guard and confused. Despite our conviction, nothing was resolved or clarified by the time the show ended. The bands and the kids all went home, and at least for the moment, that was that.

After the show, it was party time. The Wolff would soon be

heading to Bangladesh for a two year tour with the Peace Corps, and this was the last time our little group would be able to convene before he left. So convene we did, along with other leftovers from the afternoon's show. We celebrated, laughed when a cat put its head in a cup, and then the phone rang. It was Carl.

Despite any inebriation on my behalf, the conversation was completely productive. Carl explained himself, saying that the web posting wasn't about me and my friends, but rather another group of friends - the members of which he identified explicitly for the sake of clarity. I agreed – some of those kids were kind of shitty. Carl also told me that he wished I'd have come to him with this instead of standing at the helm of a public uprising; this was also difficult for me to dispute. After all, I *could* have simply asked him about it, but decided instead to let the evidence and my assumptions decide for me. Still, Carl understood how we could have thought the rant was about us, and offered every reassurance that it wasn't. The whole thing, it seemed, was really just a big misunderstanding.

While we'd been casual friends beforehand, Carl and I now bonded. Ironically, our dispute had helped each of us to gain a new level of mutual understanding - and moving forward, our friendship would grow increasingly strong. Years later I'd get married in his back yard.

Summer ended, grinding to a sudden halt much too soon as far as I was concerned. After all, here came the fall semester once again, and once again I wasn't taking classes. So I started to wonder what, exactly, I was still doing in New Brunswick, and why it seemed as if I wasn't feeling any progress in my life. Sure, my job was great and I still loved my band and my friends, but the world outside had its merits, too. Suddenly, I wanted out.

Maybe it had to be this way. I'd long heard jokes and mumblings about New Brunswick as the "city of broken dreams." And I had even witnessed myself how, for some, the town could become an infinite gray vortex, where depression and stagnation consume the meeker hearts. Maybe it had something to do with it being a college town, a place that in at least one dimension exists as a nether-region between the carefree days of youth and the compromises and daily grind of adulthood. Maybe it was because punk rock, for all of its awesomeness, still attracts fuck-ups – many of whom, no matter how intelligent or creative, never rise above the tragedy and emotional abandonment of the modern world. Maybe. Maybe. Maybe. Either way, I was finally fulfilling the promise of New Brunswick's dark cloud.

At least the irony of it all wasn't lost on me. Years ago, I embraced some vague concept of hardcore or punk rock as a life preserver, to help me stay afloat amidst the turbulence of my emotions as I tried to deal conscientiously with my suburban teenage experience. Now I'd cycled through my own path to redemption, only to arrive in a mental place where punk rock itself now seemed stifling. Sure, my friends and my band and these shows were great - but there were lots of new things I wanted to try, and most of them had absolutely nothing to do with the hardcore scene.

Somewhere in there I realized it was time for me to figure out my next real move in, like, you know – life and shit. Amidst some bizarre talk of joining the cast of MTV's *The Real World*, I ultimately decided on graduate school. Through my hippie friend Jonathan I learned of a rather unique and obnoxiously progressive teacher education program at The New School, NYC's "more radical than you" magnet. At the very least, I felt comfortable with the notion of being a professional educator. So I applied, interviewed, and was accepted for the spring semester starting that January. Just like that, I had something new to do with my life. In just a few short months, I'd be living in New York, back in school and doing something completely new and unknown.

It was something to look forward to, in a big way. The trapped feeling fell away completely, and the future actually seemed like something to be excited for; something I hadn't felt in a long time. With the pressure of life-planning now gone (at least for a short while), riding out the last few months of my time in New Brunswick suddenly sounded like a vacation. And as my impending escape drew closer each day, the stakes for me in that old city became lower and lower.

I did have mixed feelings of course. After all, I learned so much about myself and the world through my experience with hardcore and punk, and this town and its people had played a major part in that. Perspective, confidence, technical and artistic skills, and most importantly, friends – all of these things (not to mention college) had defined the last five and a half years of my life. But the real world – the one I wanted to fight and save – seemed to have become distant over time, and that really bothered me. How, exactly, was I putting my money where my mouth was? I wanted to stay sharp, and to be kept on my toes. I feared complacency, and was leery of the comforts of home. But now I had some tools, and felt ready to throw myself to the sharks. Beyond work, my band, or my cool punk rock community, I spent the fall of 1999 looking forward to a new kind of feeding frenzy.

Mike O. quit try.fail.try around this time, and Nora too. For months he'd been fucking around with some of the dudes from the legendary Jersey circus-metal band Human Remains. Though the project had been floundering for a while, they'd recently gotten their act together. Not surprisingly, the band quickly became Mike's first priority; though he was a proficient guitarist in both try.fail.try and Nora, Mike's true calling had always been the microphone. They decided to call themselves Burnt By She Sun, and they would be awesome.

Autumn blew by and grew colder, and I was busy. I needed to find a place to live in New York, as well as a replacement tenant for 20 Huntington Street who could cover what was then a relatively high rent payment of $500 a month. On top of all that, try.fail.try was about to leave for our first real tour.

I found a place to live in Greenpoint, Brooklyn, with a guy named Toby. I first met Toby in '95 or '96 outside of CBGB at a Lifetime show - I had tried to sell him a zine but wound up trading one for a copy of his own, called *Eventide*. Over the years we'd kept in touch, and now we would become roommates; *Aneurysm* may no longer have been my ambassador, but it was still influencing the course of my life. Did I know when trying to sell Toby a zine that five years we'd live together? Of course not – and to me, that was poetry.

As for the attic at 20 Huntington, I found not one but two tenants – former Purpose guitarist Mikey A., and his older brother Dan, a chemist. The only catch was that they'd have to move in weeks before I was ready to vacate. While that meant I'd spend half of December without a place of my own, I had no other choice. Ten days before Christmas, I moved all my stuff into P-Nut's Edison basement.

I spent a few days with my parents in Marlton, and then crashed on P-Nut's couch for the rest of the holiday season. There was a New Years Eve party at Vasil's house that year – a monumental gathering that has since taken on a somewhat legendary status for those who were there, or who have heard the stories. Recent research indicates that said party was, in fact, the epicenter of all documented Y2K chaos that year.

Try.fail.try (with Craig and Clay in tow) left for tour on January 2nd. Since we were smart, our first stop that icy winter was Buffalo, where after the show I argued with cops who thought the X's on our borrowed van meant that we were selling ecstasy. We then enjoyed an ice storm in Milwaukee, awesomeness in Des Moines, a completely insane 24 hours in Ohio, a band meltdown in St. Louis, and a whole lot of other shit in a bunch of other places.

After two weeks we rolled back into Jersey. Upon arrival, I had 36 hours to move and start the spring semester in a city I barely knew. And while I'd be leaving behind my truly beloved city of New Brunswick, the person I'd become there was sure to remain.

Epilogue

Soon after I moved to Brooklyn, try.fail.try hit a wall. DIY and "the revolution" had changed, and so had the environment for our style of music. But while new opportunities were beginning to emerge for heavy bands, mine – at least by the definition I assigned to it for myself - couldn't make a living for anyone. Still, try.fail.try wasn't a commune or a religion – it was a band, made of people free to change their minds. So Byrnes quit, and that was that. And while I wasn't thrilled with how the band ended, I'd grown comfortable with the notion of moving on. So I did.

Grad school was great, and I got what I wanted – a change of scenery, some new challenges, and a chance to interact with people who had absolutely nothing to do with hardcore; people who'd never heard of Easton Avenue. Any feeling of being stifled by a scene or a town quickly became a distant memory, and I was determined to explore life without the limitations I'd recently perceived as dictating my possibilities.

Yet it wasn't long before I felt like something was missing – and soon enough I found myself making regular visits to New Brunswick. Certainly, I was glad to be broadening my horizons and having new experiences in New York. But even with CBGB and ABC No Rio now in my back yard, it was simply impossible for me to beat the feeling I'd found at places like

The Melody Bar and 20 Huntington Street, the Masonic Temple and 67 Handy Street.

For me, music had become a vehicle for invoking a spirit and creating an experience. When I practiced or sang along, it was an act of defense against a world that won't slow down for anyone. At the very least, no one could take away the time I spent with my friends, loving and making music – and no one could unmake the songs I helped write, or cancel the shows where I played or danced or sang along. It made life so sweet that my teeth rot when I reminisce.

I've occasionally found this thing where people place a premium on how long someone has been down with hardcore or punk. But that's putting emphasis on messengers and ritual, as opposed to messages and meaning. At least some of us have screamed into a microphone or beaten on a guitar hoping to do more than just look cool. But the passionate few are just that - few. So I feel lucky to have encountered so many of them, in this town called New Brunswick, New Jersey. And I also feel lucky that, at least for a little while, I got to watch music prove over and over again how powerful it could be.

Don't fake the funk.

THE MR. HOLLAND'S OPUS FOUNDATION

The Mr. Holland's Opus Foundation (MHOF) supports music education and its many benefits through the donation of new and refurbished musical instruments to underserved schools, community music programs and individual students nationwide.

The Mr. Holland's Opus Foundation has served 785 music programs and individuals across the country, effectively helping thousands of students and hundreds of dedicated teachers. New and refurbished instruments with a value of $4,000,000 have been donated.

A portion of the proceeds (equaling 5% of the suggested retail price) earned by the author and Sub City Records from the sale of this release will be donated to The Mr. Holland's Opus Foundation.

mhopus.org
hopelessrecords.com
kamikazewords.com